BERKLEE

The First Fifty Years

Berklee: The First Fifty Years
Published by Berklee Press Publications
1140 Boylston Street
Boston, Massachusetts 02215-3693
USA
First Printing September 1995

Executive Editor: Lee Eliot Berk
Author: Ed Hazell
Designer: Dave Miranda
Production Supervision: Judith Lucas, Stephen Melisi

Printed by EMCO Printers
Compact discs manufacured by KAO Infosystems

I dedicate this book to Lawrence and Alma Berk, whose vision and enduring commitment I was privileged to experience from the unique vantage point of both professional colleague and son. They cherished giving educational opportunity to young people seeking careers in professional music, watching their growth, and relishing their successes. They were practicing what we today call "outcome assessment" long before higher education articulated the concept, and our college has advanced to ever higher levels of excellence and contributed much to society as a result.

Lee Eliot Berk

Boston, Massachusetts

August 21, 1995

Contents

Foreword

by President Lee Eliot Berk

I was sitting at the dinner table of a Berklee trustees meeting in October 1994. The business portion of our periodic meetings would begin about 6:30 in the evening and then continue over dinner beginning at 8 o'clock.

On this occasion, a few students had been invited, and Board of Trustees Chair Will Davis asked them to present any questions or matters they would like to air with the trustees.

One young woman remarked that the students had just received the latest edition of the *50th Anniversary News*, a publication designed to keep the Berklee community informed regarding the planning process for our 50th anniversary. She was a residence hall student, and observed that many of the students she knew didn't really understand why we were celebrating a 50th anniversary.

Her remarks stunned the trustees and many presented very expressive responses to the statement. As the discussion proceeded, we realized that many students lacked sufficient understanding and appreciation of the impressive accomplishments of Berklee in the first half-century of its existence.

As we planned our 50th anniversary celebration, I had asked that each of our highest leaders—which included myself and the deans—choose and lead an event of significance and in the spirit of the anniversary year. My choice had been the organization of a historic publication documenting the birth and development of our college. The members of every community, I had felt, deserve a knowledge of their own legacy. The questions raised by our student validated my sense of the importance of this project.

My father Lawrence Berk was the founder and first president of our college, and was subsequently appointed chancellor by the Board of Trustees upon his retirement from the presidency. He served actively from his first music education activities in 1945—from whence we date our origins—until his retirement in 1979, and thereafter as chancellor in an honorary capacity. My mother Alma Berk worked professionally at Berklee for 35 years, retiring officially in 1994 as chief public affairs officer. Much early Berklee history was residing in their offices and in their memories, and of course, in mine as well. Although I had joined Berklee professionally in the mid-1960s, I had grown up with many of the stories of the school and the challenges it had faced.

Jazz writer Ed Hazell has done a marvelous job of poring through the copious files comprising the history of Berklee, and I have done my best to assist him in the conviction that this was a particularly appropriate time to undertake this legacy project. Many of the founding and near-founding persons, who have contributed so much to the success of our college, are still with us today.

As a photo-driven historical essay, this publication is organized around available photos and stories of individuals obtaining media recognition. While this confines the book to a relatively small number of faculty, staff, alumni, and others whose public visibility provided a record of their contributions and accomplishments, the reputation of Berklee was established as well by the daily strivings and interactions of every person in the college. I want to thank all of the Berklee community, who have contributed so much in their many periods of service to our college, to education, to music, and to the world. In particular, I want to thank Graphic Designer Dave Miranda who has created an extraordinarily attractive publication presenting all the elements of the history; and Director of Publications Judith Lucas and Publications Coordinator Stephen Melisi who have managed the production process in such a caring and professional manner.

In many mature colleges, I expect there would often be constituted an official archive from which a legacy project such as this would be drawn. There might also be a college committee working as a group on such a project. This first endeavor, drawing as it does from half a century of my parents' files, was as much as I was capable of organizing. Faculty and staff were asked to contribute memorabilia, and many were consulted on an individual basis to share their memories, feelings, and impressions. An official college archive will be established in the near future. I hope that it becomes an available information resource for the next historic documentation project to be more of a shared collaborative endeavor.

Please accept, therefore, what is a sketch of a half-century of events, accomplishments, and personalities that transformed a small teaching studio into a world-class college. It is a remarkable story of commitment and creativity, and one which I believe has few, if any, parallels in higher education. Along the way, the lives of many students, faculty, and staff were endowed with a meaning that transcended any other available experience; a legitimacy in education, that previously had not existed, was extended to studies in contemporary music; and the musical accomplishments of Berklee alumni were widely acclaimed in many settings for their artistry and benefiting of humanity. We indeed have much to celebrate as we look to Berklee 2000 and the next half-century of accomplishment in the life of our college.

My wife Susan and my daughters Nancy and Lucy have shared much of my latter Berklee experience as observers, supporters, and participants. I am thankful they are with me.

2

Author's Acknowledgements

A year and a half ago, I thought Berklee was a jazz school, primarily notable for its guitarists. But in the process of writing this book, I learned that it is much, much more. I hope readers will be as surprised and delighted as I have been to learn the story of this college and how its remarkable faculty, students, and staff built it into the diverse and exciting place it is today. As President Berk notes in the foreword, this is not a complete history. But if some noteworthy Berklee personalities and campus events are missing from the book (and many are), I believe the essentials of the Berklee story are all here.

A few words about some elements of the book are in order. The time lines of landmarks in the history of jazz, rock, and music technology, although thoroughly researched, are likewise not comprehensive. They are intended to provide a context for the Berklee story and serve primarily as general indicators of events taking place outside the college. Alumni years appearing after students' names are either graduation dates or the last semester attended and are as accurate as Berklee records allow. In almost all cases, this means the year comes directly from the college's computer database. In the few instances where no record existed, alumni years were inferred, or obtained from reference books or periodicals. To avoid cluttering the text, alumni years are given only the first time former students' names appear.

I also want to thank the many people at Berklee who helped me in the course of writing this book. I especially want to thank President Lee Eliot Berk, who conceived the book and from whose guidance it benefits in many ways. Working closely with him on this project from beginning to end, I found President Berk was an unfailingly gracious and astute editor, and his memory of events at the college added many details that enrich this book.

Designer Dave Miranda also deserves enormous credit. His easy-going nature and sense of humor made putting this book together a lot of fun and his creativity make it a pleasure to see.

Behind the scenes, Director of Publications Judith Lucas and Publications Coordinator Stephen Melisi provided essential editorial support, photo research, production support, and offered valuable criticisms at several stages. Laura Kulba in the 50th Anniversary Office, and Karen Bell and Lauren Fleshler in the President's Office helped me with administrative details and were very patient with my aversion to paperwork. Executive Assistant to the President Tom Riley also read the manuscript and offered helpful suggestions and calmly handled any number of my real or imaginary crises.

Whenever I needed a fact or a lead to track something down, I turned to Director of Public Information Rob Hayes and his staff, Rob Hochschild and Allen Bush, or to Mark Small, Editor of *Berklee today,* for the answers I needed. Rob Hayes also offered helpful criticisms of the manuscript.

The contents of this book also benefit from the fruits of many people's labor. I drew heavily on a history of the Board of Trustees written by Trustee Emeritus William Falconer. Many other people were generous with their time in helping me understand the Berklee tradition and document the college's legacy. Thanks to all the faculty, administrators, and staff who took time to talk with me about the college, answered my e-mail questions and phone messages, and loaned personal photos and memorabilia for inclusion in the book.

The jazz and rock time lines were researched and prepared by a team of faculty, staff, and students including Assistant to the Performance Division Chair Rob Rose, faculty members Ken Zambello, Jackie Beard, and Jeff Stout; staff members Dorothy Messenger, Gary Haggerty, and Parker Bartlett; and students Christopher Loftlin, Sean David McGoran, and Jonathan Royal. Assistant Dean of Curriculum for Academic Technology David Mash, faculty member Tom Rhea, and Studio Manager Joe Hostetter compiled the music technology time line. Library Director John Voigt provided invaluable fact-checking and reference support for the time lines and for countless other queries.

Julie Pampinella and Chika Okamoto in the Office of the Dean of Instititional Advancement and students Alex Ball and Alex Lugo spent many hours looking up alumni years. Sarah Bodge in the Alumni Relations Office also helped with alumni research and information.

Lastly, I would like to thank my wife Ann for all her love and support during this project and for waiting until I could get away from it to go on our honeymoon.

Ed Hazell

June 1995

Prelude: 1908 – 1945

Lawrence Berk, Authorized Teacher of the Schillinger System

Born in December 1908, Lawrence Berk grew up in Boston's West End. From the age of 13, he worked professionally in music, initially as a pianist and later as a composer and arranger as well. "All through high school I worked from club to club and from theater to theater," he says. "I worked for Ruby Newman and Meyer Davis at the Copley-Plaza Hotel, and on the Ritz Carlton Roof. I worked in all the clubs as a kid when I was attending English High." He learned much of his arranger's craft first by transcribing records, then through on-the-job experience as pianist and arranger with numerous Boston-based bands and at radio stations WNAC and WEEI.

Despite his early successes and bright promise, the young Berk initially decided against a music career. "At the time, I didn't think there was much to look forward to in music and I wasn't interested in spending my life in clubs and theaters," he says. After graduating from high school in 1927, he enrolled in the prelaw program at Boston University. The next year, he transferred to Massachusetts Institute of Technology (M.I.T.) where he graduated with a degree in architectural engineering in 1932.

Lawrence Berk with the Joe Rines Orchestra, circa 1925.

4

An early shot of the Joe Rines Orchestra. Pictured are (left to right): Billy Snearson, Fred Steele, Perry Lipman, Lawrence Berk, Charlie Malenbaum, Sam Shapnick, Sam Winegrad, Peter Marcus, Tubby Lewis, and Joe Rines.

"I worked all the clubs as a kid when I was attending English High."

"Nobody wanted engineers.
So it was back to music."

He graduated from M.I.T. in the depths of the Great Depression. There were no job postings in the M.I.T. employment office that spring. "When I got through school it was the year of the deepest ebb of the Depression and nobody wanted engineers," Berk remembers. "So it was back to music."

He had worked his way through M.I.T. composing and arranging for the same orchestras he had worked for in high school—including the Joe Rines Orchestra—playing for radio broadcasts and in celebrated Hub night spots like the Mayfair, the Latin Quarter, the Metropolitan Theatre (now called the Wang Center), and the Cocoanut Grove. He worked around Boston for two more years, and then in 1934, moved to New York to further his music career.

Boston's club and theater district, Scollay Square in the 1930s.

the Boston Stein Club ... to foster the spirit of M.I.T.

As a student, Lawrence Berk was a member of the Boston Stein Club at M.I.T. The club later asked him to give a lecture on the Schillinger System at one of their meetings, and Schillinger House students performed at dances and concerts sponsored by the club.

Arriving in New York, "All I had was $17 and a tuxedo," Berk remembers. "For a while I wrote for every band I could find." Coincidentally, his former Boston employer Joe Rines moved to New York to work on the Iodent Toothpaste radio show, a big break for the band. The national exposure of commercially sponsored national radio broadcasts boosted the reputation of bands in the 1930s in the same way television appearances did in later years. Rines called Berk to write music for his new engagement. A position as staff writer/arranger for the NBC studio orchestra soon followed.

Larry Berk A R R A N G E M E N T S

1185 MORRIS AVENUE
NEW YORK CITY
JEROME 8 7742

"All I had was $17 and a tuxedo."

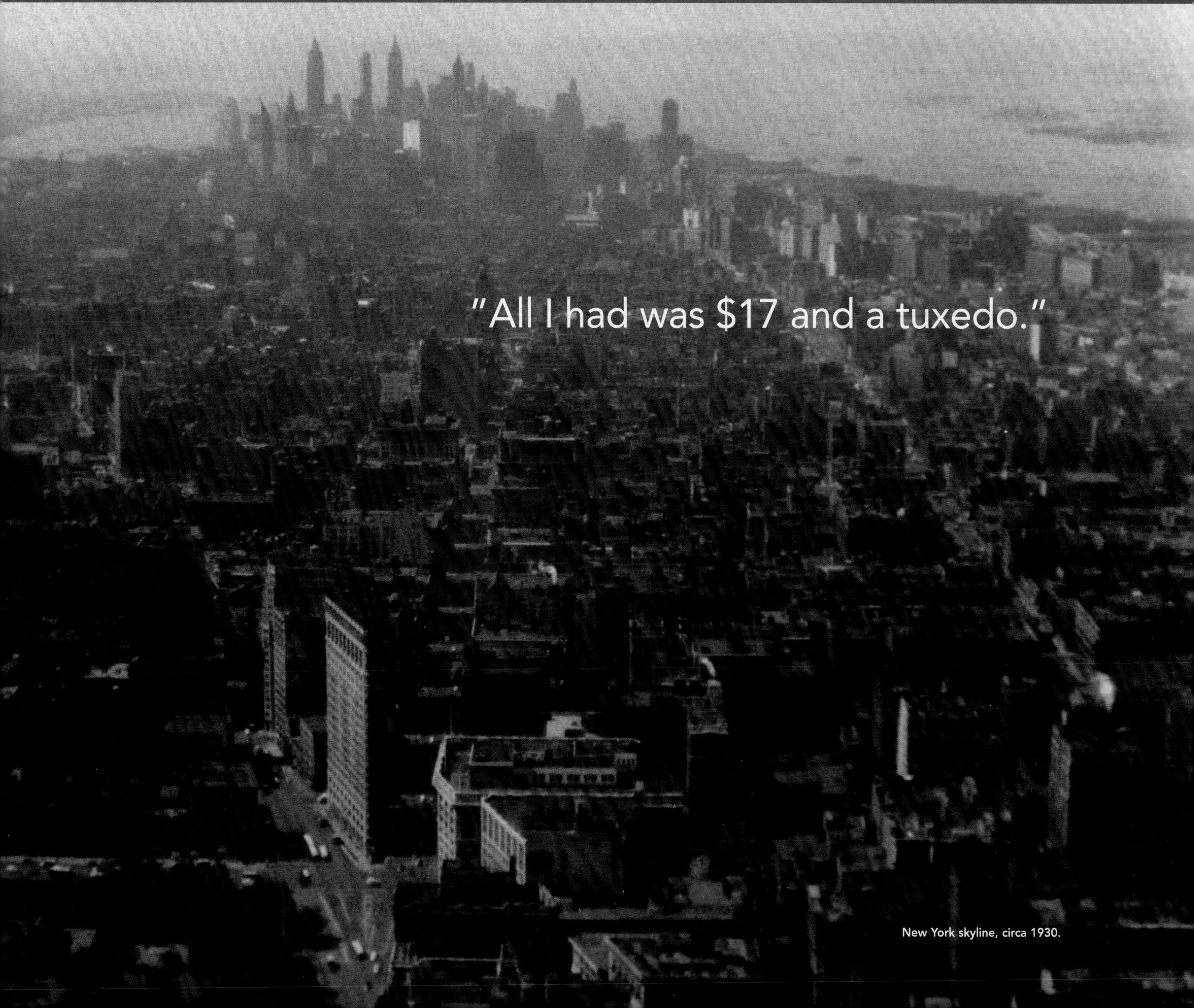

New York skyline, circa 1930.

In New York, Lawrence Berk began studying with the Russian music theorist and teacher Joseph Schillinger. Schillinger had devised a system of composition that employed mathematical permutation and combination processes to generate rhythms, harmonies, and melodies. Schillinger used graphs instead of traditional musical notation to better visualize the mathematical relationships among the constituent elements of music.

Schillinger's ideas were the subject of much debate among musicians. Berk, as both an engineer and an arranger and composer, was naturally drawn to Schillinger's ideas about music and science. He called on the reclusive composer at his Fifth Avenue apartment. Intrigued by Berk's engineering background, Schillinger agreed to take him as a student. "I paid $15 an hour to study there under Joseph Schillinger," Berk recalls. "Anyone who meant anything studied with him. All the big-name writers, composers, and network writers studied under him because he had a different approach."

Joseph Schillinger's elaborate system—the Schillinger System of Musical Composition fills two substantial volumes—did attract some very prominent students. George Gershwin composed parts of his opera *Porgy and Bess* using Schillinger's ideas. Leith Stevens used the system to compose the score to Alfred Hitchcock's *The Paradine Case*. Glenn Miller composed "Moonlight Serenade" as an exercise for a Schillinger lesson. Other students included big band leaders Benny Goodman and Tommy Dorsey, and Oscar Levant, the pianist who premiered many of Gershwin's concert pieces, and costarred as Gene Kelly's wisecracking friend in *An American in Paris*.

Although the mathematics required to use the Schillinger System were complex, during his three years of study with Schillinger, Lawrence Berk mastered the system. But it was not the specific formulas that made a lasting impression. Berk came away with a great respect for Schillinger's general thought process and the belief that a focused application of some of his ideas could be used by almost any musician in many areas of commercial writing and arranging.

As World War II loomed, Berk returned to Boston and gave up his musical career to put his engineering degree to use in the war effort. "When World War II broke out, the government was clamoring for people with engineering backgrounds," he says. He went to work for Raytheon and later became head of the mechanical design section working on radar receivers. But he was discontented. "I disliked being divorced from music after having spent so many years at it," he says.

Joseph Schillinger.

Some prominent students of Joseph Schillinger: Tommy Dorsey, Oscar Levant, Benny Goodman, Glenn Miller, and Joe Rines.

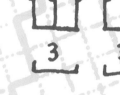
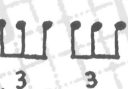

4/4 (2)

4/4 (3)

(4)

(5)

4/4 (6)

4/4 (7)

4/4 (8)

11

After Joseph Schillinger died in 1943, Lawrence Berk was among the dozen teachers, sometimes called "the 12 disciples," who were officially sanctioned to teach the Schillinger System.

In the early 1940s, Lawrence Berk began teaching the Schillinger System part-time in a studio he rented at the Loew's State Theater, located at 209 Massachusetts Avenue. Now demolished, the theater stood just a few blocks down the street from the current location of the school's major campus building. He was reluctant to give up his Raytheon position for a teaching career because he now had a family to support. In 1936, he had married the former Alma Schlager. Their son Lee was born in 1942. Since he had time to teach only on Saturday afternoons, he took just three students.

He found he enjoyed teaching. His students responded to his practical advice, based on his experiences as a working professional musician. He recalled the difficulties he and his circle of fellow musicians faced in developing their talents because there were no organized sources of information that could help them. He wanted to give his students the opportunity for organized study that he missed as a young musician.

The effectiveness of his teaching, his reputation as a successful New York composer and arranger, and his knowledge of the difficult Schillinger System, helped build his reputation. "I was at an advantage, having gone to M.I.T.," he says. "I simplified [Schillinger's] theories so the unoriented music student could use them effectively."

The number of students wanting to study with him grew larger. "What these musicians were able to do and the excitement they created developed a waiting list," Berk remembers. So he left his job at Raytheon, hoping he could support his family on a full-time schedule of $5-an-hour lessons. He needn't have worried. Soon he wasn't able to handle the teaching load by himself and he needed to recruit the best of his former students to join him as teachers.

The time seemed right to expand his teaching practice, with the waiting list of students, and a growing demand for music instruction created by the armed forces musicians returning from World War II.

He talked over the idea of starting a music school with his wife Alma. "I was probably getting impossible to live with because Alma agreed quickly," he says. "She insisted that if I wanted to teach music, then I should do it or I'd never be happy." He purchased a three-story building at 284 Newbury Street at the corner of Gloucester Street, and opened Schillinger House in 1945. It was originally a center for Lawrence Berk's independent teaching studio. He also rented private studio space in the building to musicians such as saxophonist Joe Viola, drummer Sam Tully, trumpeter Fred Berman, and many others who became early Schillinger House faculty. As Lawrence Berk's teaching load increased, he asked more of the resident musicians to handle some of the classes.

"I never expected to start a school at all," Berk told the *Boston Globe* in 1993. "Talented kids seemed to find me and I got busier and my best students became teachers and that's how the school started."

Lawrence Berk
former NBC and CBS arranger has been appointed

AUTHORIZED TEACHER
OF THE SCHILLINGER SYSTEM

of Arranging and Composition by the

Schillinger Society of New York

THE SCHILLINGER SOCIETY

INTERVIEW BY APPOINTMENT ONLY

Commonwealth 5204

Beacon 5441
Room 42

Avenue, Boston, Mass.

284 Newbury Street in the late 1950s, after Schillinger House became the Berklee School of Music.

Chapter One

Schillinger House
1945 – 1954

In 1945, as World War II ended, a relieved United States returned to a normal, peacetime life. Families relaxed at home to music on the radio. Television was a relative curiosity. The record-buying public listened to fragile 78 rpm records, but the 33 1/3 rpm long-playing record and the 45 rpm single were only a few years away. Jazz was the music of the day. Although big bands featuring singers as star attractions still filled the nightclubs and the airwaves, they were enjoying their final days as the nation's favorite dance music. In New York, Charlie Parker, Dizzy Gillespie, Kenny Clarke, Thelonious Monk, and a handful of others were fomenting the bebop revolution that would help transform jazz into a music played by small groups primarily for listening. Rhythm and blues artists were sowing the seeds for a new kind of dance music that would be called rock and roll.

In Boston, Lawrence Berk was hard at work establishing his new school, Schillinger House. He started by building a faculty that could help him realize his special vision of music education. In less than 10 years, Schillinger House became widely known to students and professional musicians alike as an innovative school for jazz and contemporary music.

Lawrence Berk at the blackboard with students Dick Nash '48, Frank Vivino '48, and Tommy Furtado '49. Note Schillinger System graph in upper right of blackboard.

Jazz	**1945**	Dizzy Gillespie forms his first big band.	Charlie Parker records "Koko" and "Now's the Time."	Woody Herman forms his first Herd.	Lionel Hampton records "Hey-Ba-Ba-Re-Bop."	Pete Rugolo joins Stan Kenton.
Rock/Pop	**1945**	Erskine Hawkins records "Caldonia."	Earl Scruggs joins Bill Monroe and the Blue Grass Boys.	Arthur Smith records "Guitar Boogie" on a Fender electric guitar.	
Technology	**1945**	John Hanert develops his Electrical Orchestra.	Musique Concréte developed in Paris.		

Among the first faculty Berk hired was a saxophonist who had come to him, fresh out of the army, to learn the Schillinger System. His name was Joe Viola, and 50 years later, he was still an active member of the Berklee community.

A lead alto for several dance orchestras before the war, Viola could communicate his knowledge and experience to both advanced students and beginners. He immediately assumed a variety of duties. "In the beginning we all worked in various areas of instruction," he once told an interviewer. "Departments as such didn't exist. Actually, most of my work in those early years involved teaching theory classes, composition, ensembles, and applied saxophone, clarinet, and flute. I taught the bulk of the ensembles at the Schillinger House, and later Berklee School of Music, for 12 years or so." He retired as chair of the Woodwind Department in 1985, but continued giving private lessons.

Viola earned widest renown as a private instructor. He placed special emphasis on achieving a good, strong sound and urged all his students to double on at least one other instrument. When asked to name his most important teacher, former Berklee faculty member and jazz saxophonist Charlie Mariano '51 told *Wind Player* magazine, "Joe Viola, head of the reed department at Berklee College in Boston. I had just gotten out of the army, and I'd been playing about six years; my sound was pretty small. Joe really made me aware, helped me to produce a big tone."

When asked what he thought was the secret to his popularity among his students, Viola replied, "I really enjoy teaching and I take a sincere interest in my students. To me, that's my job! I'm very concerned with what they do as a player; I really am."

Student saxophonist Charlie Mariano (standing, extreme left) and faculty member Joe Viola (standing with alto) play during the 1951 annual concert.

1946 Charlie Parker records "Ornithology" and "Lover Man" for Dial.

Woody Herman records Stravinsky's "Ebony Concerto."

1946 Louis Jordan records "Let the Good Times Roll."

Nat "King" Cole records "The Christmas Song."

Joe Viola conducts a student ensemble as Supervisor of Brass Instruction Fred Berman (left), Lawrence Berk (second from left), and bandleader Charlie Spivak observe.

"I take a sincere interest in my students. To me, that's my job!"
Joe Viola

Robert Share (left) and Duke Ellington examine a score during Duke's visit to the school in 1957.

Robert Share, pianist Dave Brubeck, and Lawrence Berk, circa 1961.

Robert Share on a college jazz band competition jury.

In 1945, Lawrence Berk hired another former student who would play an important role in the school—Robert Share. At 17, Share was one of Lawrence Berk's first three students at his Massachusetts Avenue studio. He remained with the school until his death in 1984.

Share taught Schillinger System, theory, harmony, and scoring. By all accounts he was an excellent teacher. Current Dean of Curriculum Gary Burton '62, who learned harmony from him as a student in the early 1960s, says, "Bob Share's class organized harmony for me. And I wasn't alone. The people who went on to create our Harmony Department all learned their harmony from Bob Share."

Like so many faculty, Share had many other responsibilities. As Berklee administrator from 1966 to 1979, and then as provost from 1979 to 1984, he was responsible for near-ly every aspect of the day-to-day operation of the school, from ordering new blackboards to curriculum development and from supervising the *Jazz in the Classroom* recordings to administering Berklee Press. "He and Larry were a great team," Professor of Jazz Composition Herb Pomeroy '52 remembers. "Larry was the guy to take the chances; he had the vision. Bob knew how to put Larry's ideas into action."

Share was also an important Berklee ambassador to other schools and colleges, serving as a judge to collegiate jazz festivals and high school jazz competitions around the country. "He was the best judge at any collegiate jazz festival I ever participated in," says Pomeroy. "He had great insight into the music and an ability to verbalize what he was feeling and write it into his critiques. He was superb, intelligent, musical, and able to express himself."

1947 Mario Bauza and Machito Orchestra create first Latin jazz.	Cuban percussionist Chano Pozo joins Dizzy Gillespie.	Charlie Parker records "Scrapple from the Apple."	Dexter Gordon records tenor battle with Wardell Gray.
		1947 Ahmet Ertegun forms Atlantic Records.	Chess Records formed.
		1947 Full-track monophonic tape recorders marketed.	

Richard Bobbitt, Lawrence Berk, and Robert Share.

Lawrence Berk's third critical early hire was Richard Bobbitt. Dr. Bobbitt taught scoring and the Schillinger System, then left for several years to earn his Ed.D. and serve as dean of Boston Conservatory of Music. After he returned to Berklee in 1963 as dean, he was an effective advocate on behalf of Berklee's contemporary music education program to accreditation association representatives who were more familiar with traditional music education approaches. He was also a leader in shaping the Music Education Department and in introducing the General Education Department into the curriculum. He retired in 1985 and was appointed dean emeritus.

Dr. Richard Bobbitt (left) analyzes a student score on an overhead projector as Voice of America broadcaster Willis Conover watches.

Bud Powell records "Bud's Bubble." | Louis Armstrong forms All-Stars. | **1948** Woody Herman records Ralph Burns' "Early Autumn."

1948 Wynonie Harris releases R&B hit "Good Rockin' Tonight." | John Lee Hooker records "Boogie Children."

1949 Lennie Tristano records "Subconscious-Lee."

Miles Davis records *Birth of the Cool.*

George Shearing forms quintet.

Charlie Parker records with Machito.

1949 Hank Williams releases first #1 country hit "Lovesick Blues."

Billboard changes "Race Records" chart to "Rhythm and Blues."

Fats Domino records his first million-selling record "The Fat Man."

1949 33 1/3 rpm long-playing records marketed.

Besides enlisting faculty, Lawrence Berk faced a second challenge. With a mortgage, overhead costs, and a faculty payroll to meet, he needed to devote more effort to building enrollment. He hoped students would be attracted by a course of study that was both practical and broad-based. Composed exclusively of "musical subjects, theoretical, practical, and applied," the curriculum, according to the 14-page 1946 catalog, was designed for a wide range of interests: "From the writer of popular songs to the symphonist, from the arranger of tunes for dance band to the orchestrator of television and moving picture scores, from the composer of radio jingles to the creator of tone poems."

Founded "upon the belief that the present-day aspirant to a career in music, faced with the most savage competition yet known, must receive the ultimate in training in order to succeed," the catalog promised quick results. A concentration on musical subjects, "together with a unique blend of the practical laboratory approach and a scientific method of instruction, enables students to produce work of a very high caliber as early as the first semester of training."

The first year, there were less than 50 students preparing themselves for "savage competition." But by 1947, classes were conducted on a full-time basis and Lawrence Berk assumed full-time administrative duties.

THE FOUR-YEAR DIPLOMA COURSE

AT

schillinger house

BOSTON'S PROGRESSIVE SCHOOL OF MUSIC

THE FACULTY COMMITTEE OFFERS SIX SCHOLARSHIPS IN THE DIPLOMA COURSE COMPRISING COLLEGIATE LEVEL FULL TIME STUDY. IN THE FIELD OF MUSIC, INCLUDING THE SCHILLINGER SYSTEM OF ARRANGING AND COMPOSITION, PARTICIPATION IN ENSEMBLES OF PROFESSIONAL CALIBRE, AND PRIVATE INSTRUMENTAL INSTRUCTION UNDER MASTER TUTORS.

TWO FULL SCHOLARSHIPS of $300.00 each, the full tuition fee for one semester.

TWO PART SCHOLARSHIPS of $150.00 each.

TWO PART SCHOLARSHIPS of $100.00 each.

THESE SCHOLARSHIPS HAVE BEEN ESTABLISHED FOR TALENTED MEMBERS OF THE GRADUATING CLASS IN QUALIFIED HIGH AND PREPARATORY SCHOOLS. CANDIDATES FOR SCHOLARSHIP AWARDS ARE REQUESTED TO FORWARD RECOMMENDATIONS FROM THEIR PRINCIPAL OR MUSIC DIRECTOR AT THE TIME OF APPLICATION. EVALUATION OF QUALIFICATIONS AND APPOINTMENT TO A SCHOLARSHIP WILL BE MADE BY THE SCHILLINGER HOUSE FACULTY COMMITTEE ON SCHOLARSHIPS.

IF INTERESTED IN ANY OF THE ABOVE SCHOLARSHIPS OR IN THE STUDY OF MUSIC WRITE

Brass students on the steps of Schillinger House. Supervisor of Brass Instruction Fred Berman stands at the head of the group (second from right, holding a newspaper).

The rapid rise in full-time enrollment was largely due to an influx of students on the GI Bill. Widely regarded as the most important veterans' legislation ever passed, the Serviceman's Readjustment Act, popularly known as the GI Bill of Rights, provided a monthly subsistence allowance and paid school expenses for nearly eight million World War II veterans. Obtaining authorization to accept students on the GI Bill was a major accomplishment for the school.

Most of the veterans on the GI Bill were already practicing musicians. One ex-GI, pianist Dean Earl '54, later a Berklee professor, entered Schillinger House in 1950 because, "I just wanted to be more reliable on the bandstand," he says. Already a busy professional, Earl remembers, "I used to work all night and take the train back from Portland [Maine] or the Cape [Cod] to catch Bob Share's harmony class. Most of the students at the school were like that, too."

24

Dean Earl, in his last semester as a student at the Berklee School of Music in 1954, plays piano at the Hi Hat club, located on the corner of Columbus Street and Massachusetts Avenue, with jazz saxophone great Sonny Stitt, and Boston-area musicians, drummer Marquis Foster and bassist Bernie Griggs.

1950 Stan Kenton forms 43-piece Innovations in Modern Music Orchestra.

Woody Herman forms his Third Herd.

Parker and Gillespie record *Bird and Diz* for Verve.

1950 The Weavers record "Good Night, Irene."

Patti Page records "The Tennessee Waltz."

Nat "King" Cole records "Mona Lisa."

1950 Les Paul develops multitrack recording using Ampex tape recorder.

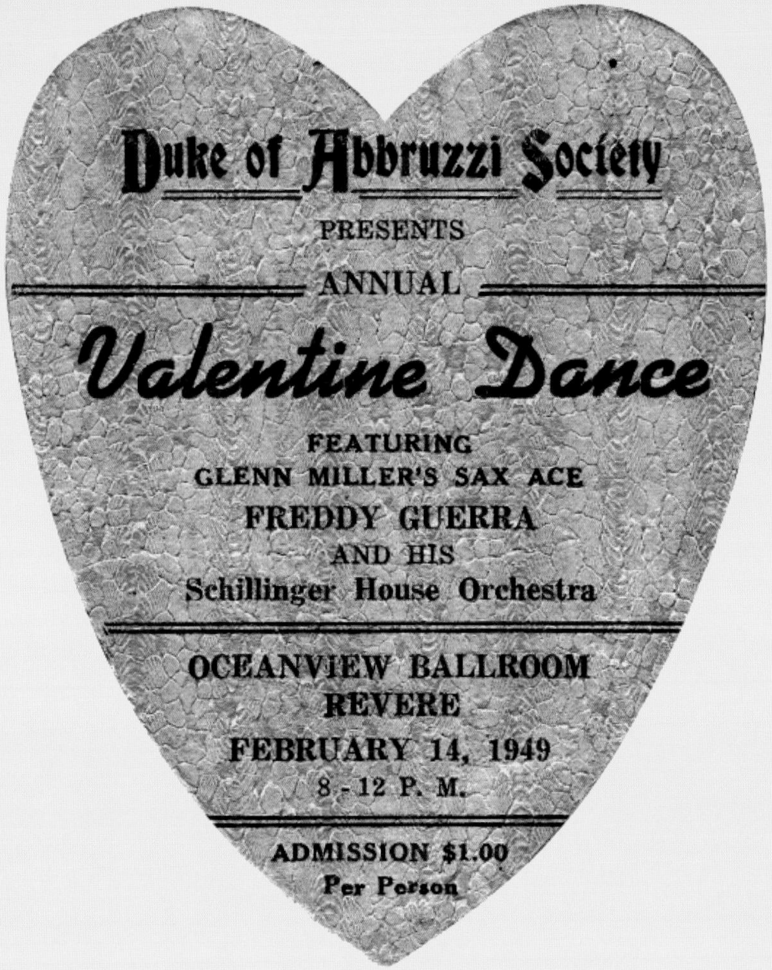

Duke of Abbruzzi Society

PRESENTS

ANNUAL

Valentine Dance

FEATURING
GLENN MILLER'S SAX ACE
FREDDY GUERRA
AND HIS
Schillinger House Orchestra

OCEANVIEW BALLROOM
REVERE
FEBRUARY 14, 1949
8 - 12 P. M.

ADMISSION $1.00
Per Person

Two Schillinger House dance orchestras were created in 1948. The Schillinger House orchestras gave students the chance to play in professional situations at functions and dances throughout the Boston area and generated visibility for the school. Joe Viola led one band, Freddie Guerra the other. Guerra had been in Glenn Miller's Army Air Force Orchestra in Europe during the war. He began teaching saxophone and ensemble at Schillinger House in 1946.

schillinger house
204 NEWBURY STREET · BOSTON, MASS

'48

Spring Dance

Joe Viola leads a Schillinger House orchestra at the Hotel Continental, Cambridge, in 1948.

The Spring Dance, featuring student orchestras led by Freddy Guerra and Joe Viola.

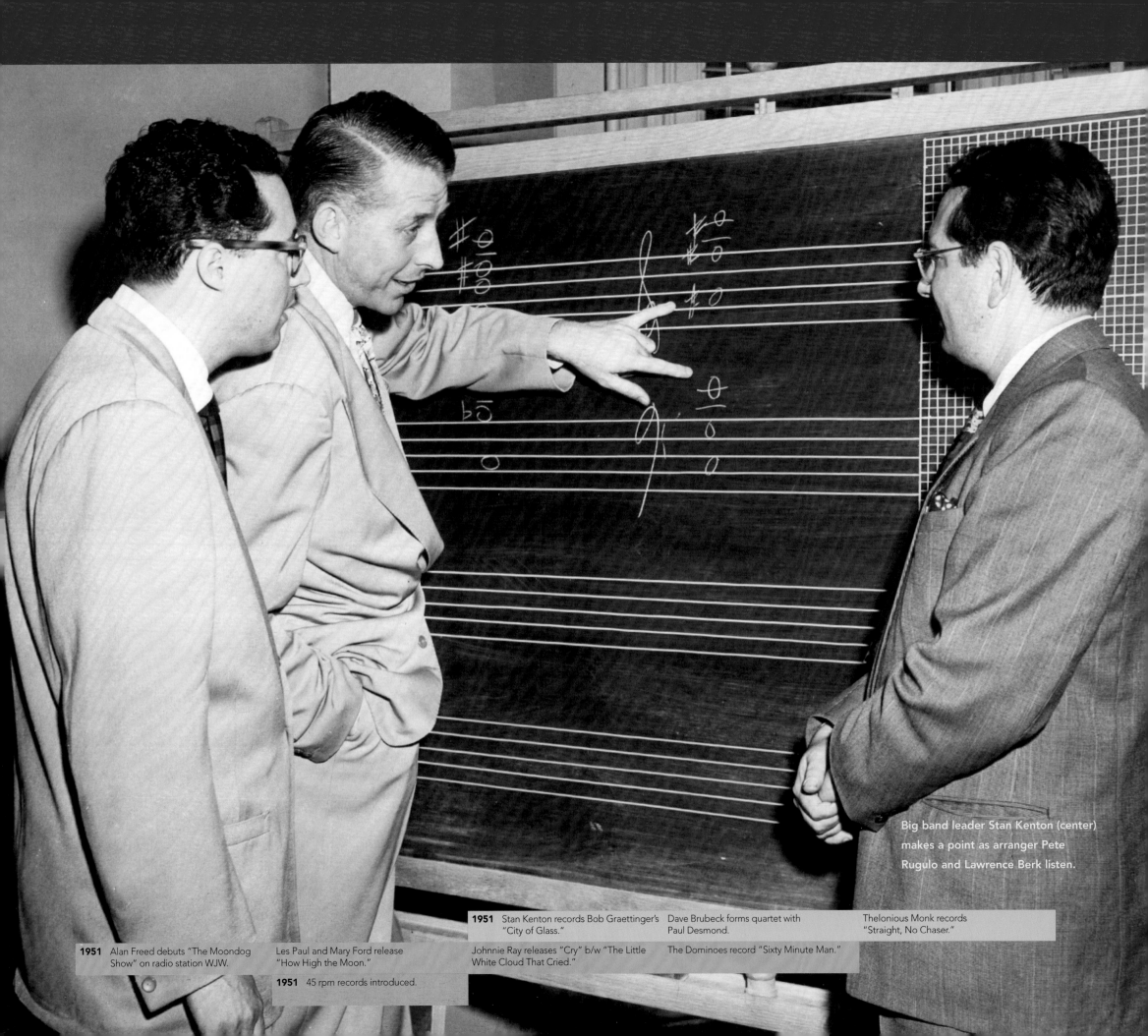

Big band leader Stan Kenton (center) makes a point as arranger Pete Rugulo and Lawrence Berk listen.

1951 Stan Kenton records Bob Graettinger's "City of Glass."

Dave Brubeck forms quartet with Paul Desmond.

Thelonious Monk records "Straight, No Chaser."

1951 Alan Freed debuts "The Moondog Show" on radio station WJW.

Les Paul and Mary Ford release "How High the Moon."

Johnnie Ray releases "Cry" b/w "The Little White Cloud That Cried."

The Dominoes record "Sixty Minute Man."

1951 45 rpm records introduced.

WOODY HERMAN TOPS STAN KENTON IN
SCHILLINGER HOUSE POLL
Burns Noses Out Rugolo As Top Arranger

LARGE BAND

1. Woody Herman.....................200
2. Stan Kenton.......................96
3. Dizzy Gillespie....................40
4. Duke Ellington.....................24
5. Les Brown.........................20

SMALL BAND

1. Charlie Parker....................120
2. King Cole..........................96
3. Charlie Ventura....................92
4. Goodman Sextet.....................32
5. Dizzy Gillespie....................24
6. Joe Mooney.........................20
6. Art Tatum..........................20

ARRANGER

1. Ralph Burns.......................132
2. Pete Rugolo.......................100
3. Eddie Sauter.......................44
4. Sy Oliver..........................28
5. Duke Ellington.....................24
6. Tadd Dameron.......................20
6. Frank DeVol........................20

INSTRUMENTALIST

1. Charlie Parker.....................80
2. Benny Goodman......................44
3. Dizzy Gillespie....................44
4. Lennie Tristano....................36
5. Art Tatum..........................32
6. Tommy Dorsey.......................20

CLASSICAL COMPOSER

1. Igor Stravinsky...................148
2. Claude Debussy.....................88
3. Rimsky-Korsakov....................24

A 1949 poll published in the first issue of the student newspaper *The Score* shows the Schillinger House students had their fingers on the pulse of modern jazz.

In 1949, Schillinger House attracted even more students by adding a Music Education major to majors in Arranging, Composition, and Applied Music. That same year, branch studios opened in Worcester and Springfield, Massachusetts, and remained active for several years. In March 1949, Berk could tell *Metronome* magazine there were over 500 Schillinger House students and their ranks were growing. "It's not just a matter of getting new music students. Ninety percent of our enrollment is made up of transfer students who were studying elsewhere and who heard what we were doing," he said to reporter George Simon.

Students, teachers, arrangers, conductors and composers of music in all its forms:

schillinger house
284 NEWBURY STREET · BOSTON, MASS.

announces the opening of
BRANCH STUDIOS in WORCESTER
on July 28, 1947, at 306 Main St.

AUTHORIZED TEACHER
SCHILLINGER SYSTEM

Students may specialize in
DANCE BAND ARRANGING:

I. Harmonic devices; high-tension chords.
II. Rhythmic devices; evolution of complete range of swing patterns.
III. Improvization.
IV. Four-way writing.
V. Five-way writing.
VI. Voicings; sectional and ensemble.
VII. Reharmonization.
VIII. Layout; preparation of complete orchestral scores for professional use.

Mr. Lawrence Berk, regional representative of the Schillinger Society in New York and director of Schillinger House in Boston will give interviews by appointment.

Phone: WORCESTER 6-2086

SCHILLINGER HOUSE STUDENTS MAKE GRADE WITH NAME ORKS

Chicago, December 15, 1950

Ten Alumni Have Recently Been Added To Top Rosters

By 1949, Lawrence Berk's efforts to build the school and its reputation were beginning to meet increasing success. *Down Beat* and *Metronome* magazines regularly ran glowing stories about the school. Nationally prominent bandleaders and musicians started to visit the school when they were in Boston. Stan Kenton made the first of many stops he would make over the years in 1949. On his 1950 visit, bandleader Count Basie said he approved of Berk's innovative undertaking.

"A great future awaits musicians who can arrange," Basie was quoted in a local paper. "Just as the 'Great American Novel' has not been written, similarly in music, the ultimate has not been reached. Sidemen who can also arrange add to their incomes as well as improve their musicianship. I wholeheartedly approve of the Schillinger System of Arranging as taught at Schillinger House School of Music in Boston."

Count Basie (right) examines a student score with Kenneth MacKillop, Jr., (left) the first dean of Schillinger House, during a 1950 visit. MacKillop was a former public school administrator and musician. Students called him "the joking professor" for his humor and effervescent personality. He left Berklee in 1955 for a position at his alma mater, Tufts University.

1952 Gerry Mulligan and Chet Baker form pianoless quartet.

The Modern Jazz Quartet records "Vendome" and "La Ronde."

Jazz at the Philharmonic to Europe.

1952 Alan Freed produces first rock and roll concert.

Jimmy Forrest records "Night Train."

1952 Les Paul uses custom-made Ampex 8 tape recorder.

Master of Ceremonies Lawrence Berk at the first annual concert, "A Montage of Modern Music," held at John Hancock Hall in 1950.

Drum teacher Sam Tully (right) and a student play cash registers during the "Filene's Basement" movement of *Boston Jig-Saw.*

BOSTON JIG-SAW

A City Set To Music

Listen, the man said, while the city sings . . . .

Listen to the far-off growl of trolley cars, the whisper of the wind around tall buildings, the aching call of a freight engine after midnight, the distant signalling of the fish boats as they start out from "T" Wharf at the crack of dawn. . . .Listen for the dissonances in traffic, the bleat of taxi horns and under it all the mumble of talking people, hundreds, thousands of talking people, talking about the weather, business, the moon, the stars, love, a million things. . . .for that's the way the city sings.

People who come here to Schillinger House to learn things are always listening. That's what music is, the listening, and then the telling of what you heard down in that little secret pocket of your mind, that little pocket which made you want to be a musician in the first place.

So the man said listen to Boston. . . .listen with your ears, your minds, your hearts.

And that's what this is, the things our young men heard, then wove together into a series of little musical sketches, a piece of music we call. . . .

Boston Jig-saw. . . .

So lend us your ears for a little while. Pretend maybe that you are a boy or a girl, that you are in love, and let us take you with music this Spring day on a tour of our home town.

THE PUBLIC GARDENS.

Physicists will tell you that color vibrates in tune with musical notes, that one day a composer will write in terms of light, color and tone. . . .and that's the way it is in the Public Gardens in Spring, when the tulip beds are glorious high notes in a minor symphony of loveliness, softened by the deep green of proud trees, the soft suppliance of weeping willows. The Swan Boats pass slowly in review before gay people, star-scattered on the grass. . . . and beyond, the Ritz pokes its elegance toward the sky.

FILENE'S BASEMENT.

Hell hath no fury like a woman scorned. . . .except in a bargain basement like Filene's where you really learn that the female is more deadly than the male! Yes, madam. No, madam, it doesn't come in that size. They're here today and gone tomorrow, madam. You should have been here yesterday. Baby shoes, two aisles to the right. . . .and so it goes in pleasant cacaphony, punctuated by the jingling of cash registers singing their own little theme of business, business, business. And it's a good thing. Here are women, hundreds of women, going about their business, running their homes, trying to save a little, make a little. So it is in Boston. And so it is in free America.

6

Boston Jig-Saw painted musical portraits of six different Boston landmarks. The narration was written by *Boston Daily Record* columnist George W. Clarke.

Dean MacKillop (left) and student composer Kendall Capps, Jr., (right) present a recording of *Boston Jig-Saw* to Boston Mayor John Hynes (center). After working in Hollywood for many years, Capps returned as the first chair of the Film Scoring Department at Berklee in 1969.

On April 30, 1950, students gathered at John Hancock Hall for the first of many annual spring concerts, called "A Montage of Modern Music." The event showcased the work of student composers and arrangers in the diverse styles taught at the school. In order to give every student a chance to play, the programs frequently lasted for up to four hours. "Larry liked to give people their money's worth," Joe Viola says of these mammoth productions.

The highlight of the 1950 program, which featured seven ensembles, each playing three or more selections, was *Boston Jig-Saw: A City Set to Music.* Five students composed the six-part work that painted a musical portrait of a different Boston landmark—the Public Gardens, the corner of Tremont and Boylston streets, Fenway Park, the Fish Pier, Filene's Basement, and Harvard Yard. William Leavitt, later the chair of Berklee's Guitar Department from 1966 to 1990, and Kendall Capps, Jr., the first chair of the Film Scoring Department, were two of the student composers. In the program book, *Boston Daily Record* columnist George W. Clarke described the "Filene's Basement" movement this way: "Hell hath no fury like a woman scorned . . . except in a bargain basement like Filene's where you really learn that the female is more deadly than the male! Yes, madam. No, madam, it doesn't come in that size. Baby shoes, two aisles to the right. . . . And so it goes in pleasant cacophony, punctuated by the jingling of cash registers singing their own little theme of business, business, business." Shortly after the concert, a recording of the work was presented to Boston Mayor John Hynes.

33

TELEVISION WEEK 10¢

Complete
TV Programs   DEC. 6 TO DEC. 12

Stars Of Tomorrow
SEE PAGE 8

Community
OPTICIANS

JONES: Thanks, Vern . . . I am sure your good advise will be acted on by very many of our wonderful audience at home. (Introduce first, second and third of last show)

CUE: APPLAUSE

JONES: Sings four bars then hums during closing spiel

VERN: ON CUE: Friends, if you would likt to see COMMUNITY AUDITIONS as actually telecast from the WBZ-TV theatre, send your request for tickets now to:

        COMMUNITY AUDITIONS
        BOX A - ESSEX STATION
        BOSTON, MASS.

Z And make it a date for sure, be with us ____ weeks from today _____ to see another wonderful contest of amateurs.

Until then -- this is Vern Williams, reminding you that most people buy glasses at Community Opticians for Qua. that is high, prices that ae low, service that is frie and credit that is just as easy as you wish.

Yes, you can place your confidence in COMMUNITY OPTIC.

In August 1950, Lawrence Berk announced that Schillinger House would help produce an amateur talent contest called "Community Auditions," on television station WBZ. Sponsored by Community Opticians, a major Boston-area eyewear retailer, and hosted by Gene Jones and Vernon Williams, the weekly program would prove to be one of the most popular locally produced shows in New England television history. "Here's further proof that the fame and competence of the school have earned the recognition and confidence of the public," *Metronome* magazine said.

Each week, Schillinger House faculty auditioned local talent and selected six acts to appear on a live, Sunday afternoon broadcast. In 1952, Lawrence Berk estimated almost 3,500 applicants were screened. The enormous task of auditioning and selecting talent fell primarily to Supervisor of the Piano Department Harry Smith and piano teacher Lee Daniels. Both had extensive experience in local radio studios and musical theater. Smith, along with bass instructor William Curtis, and drum instructor Sam Tully, usually accompanied the acts on-air. Viewers could vote for their favorite talent by postcard. Although Berklee involvement ended in the late 1960s, the show remained on WBZ until 1986.

1953 Mulligan, Baker, and Konitz record "Revelations."   Bud Powell records "Glass Enclosure."   Horace Silver records "Opus de Funk."

1953 Willie Mae "Big Mama" Thornton records "Hound Dog."   The Orioles record "Crying in the Chapel."

1953 Stereophonic sound accompanies 3-D Cinemascope and Cinerama movies.

A contestant sings on "Community Auditions." The pianists are Schillinger House teachers Harry Smith and Lee Daniels. Host Verne Williams sits at right.

Singer Teddi King appears on "Tune Tryouts" with a Schillinger House orchestra under the direction of Freddy Guerra.

Singer Teddi King.

Encouraged by the success of "Community Auditions," Lawrence Berk also created a second amateur talent show, "Tune Tryouts," a songwriting contest for amateur composers. As in the case of "Community Auditions," Schillinger House provided musicians and arrangements and selected material for broadcast. Each week, the three songs judged best by Schillinger faculty were performed on the program. Viewers voted by postcard for their favorite song and every fifth show, the previous four winners competed against each other. Sheet music of the song voted best by the public was published. Schillinger House averaged 80 entries each week and WBZ tabulated over 6,000 weekly viewer postcard votes. Freddy Guerra recorded some of the songs and the records received local air play.

Singer Rudy Vallee appeared as a special guest one week, but the show's regular vocalist was a Schillinger student named Teddi King. Just a year after the show debuted, pianist George Shearing heard her at the Stables and asked her to join his band. Primarily a jazz singer, she enjoyed cross-over success in the pop market in the late 1950s.

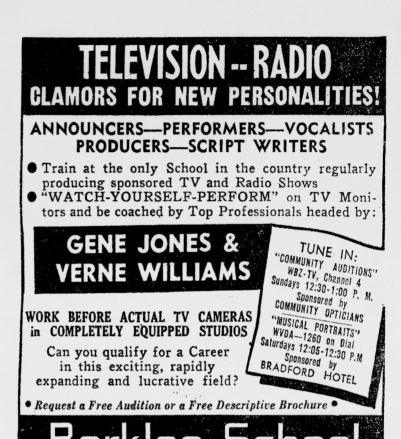

With the ongoing popularity of "Community Auditions" and the rapid growth of the television industry, writing, arranging, and performing for television became part of the Schillinger House curriculum. The school equipped a television studio so students could get the hands-on training that was the cornerstone of the school's educational approach. Advertisements emphasized that students learned through the "Watch-Yourself-Perform" method, whereby they can see themselves working on television monitors."

Under the direction of instructor Lee Daniels (sitting on left), "Community Auditions" winner, seven-year-old Phil Phillips practices while Robert Share operates the camera.

1954 The first Newport Jazz Festival.   Sonny Rollins and Miles Davis record
                                                   "Airegin" and "Oleo."

1954 Elvis Presley records first Sun Records   Big Joe Turner records "Shake, Rattle,   Bill Haley and His Comets record "(We're
          session.   and Roll."   Gonna) Rock Around the Clock."

THE ROARING TWENTIES

THE FLAPPER

She walked in hobbles like a penguin on parade, skipping gutters with a quick one-two, and when she stood at ease, they called it the "Debutante Slouch." Any hat that did not hide her eyes was not de rigeur, and the man of her dreams somehow managed to look a lot like Rudolph Valentino; her ivory tower was a silken tent in a desert where the sands were golden and the sky at night was like black velvet, studded with diamonds..... When she danced it was to a Charleston beat, raucous, brassy, graceless. But love was the same then as it is now....and she was the same warm-hearted girl that her daughter is today....pledging the eternal vows in a darkened vestibule, thinking of the wonder of a home and family of her own....with irate papa, of course, shouting from the head of the stairs. Because yesterday's flapper is your own mother. Hi, mom!

LIFE AND DEATH OF A GANGSTER

Death roared down the highways in the fantastic 20's, crept into alleys, lay in wait at street corners....invaded the tall shining buildings and grubby tenements alike. Because the "Thou-shalt-nots" had passed a law, a law which spawned a brood of evil opportunists who delivered the goods in camouflaged trucks, powerful motorboats running in the darkness with muffled engines....the jackals who preyed on the rebellious desires of an America who refused to be legislated. The killers came....striking swiftly and remorselessly, retreating to their hideaways to emerge again to the chorus of stuttering Tommy guns. It was a game of cops and robbers....played for keeps, with the Reaper as the umpire....the obituary written by a hot trumpet wailing an obbligato to the Death March.

HELLO, SUCKER!

Nightlife was spelled T-E-X-A-S G-U-I-N-A-N in the Roarin' Twenties.... not that she was beautiful, not that she was talented, not that she was rich. She was none of those things. But she was human. And for all the glare and glitter, the razzle and the dazzle, people were lonely....and so she became the High Priestess of the Fun Cult, the uncrowned queen of glamor gulch, who wore the lights of Broadway like a tiara in her hair! Her little gals were prettier than others, and "Give the little girl a hand!" crept into the English language. Tex's throne was the back of a cafe chair, and, with her feet on the seat, there she'd sit like an empress, and the Broadwayfarer, the wise guy, the very one who knew all the answers, deemed himself touched with a royal accolade if she recognized his presence with the words: "Hello, Sucker!" For that was fame, as phoney as the diamond on his finger....So she epitomized the irony of the age --- "Hello, Sucker!"

THE BIG CRASH

Everyone knew that two chickens waited for every pot, that every garage was really intended for two cars, and that stocks, any stocks, were really worth twice the price, no matter what the price was. It was the day of the twenty-four hour millionaire, the plunger, the pyramiding genius whose accomplishments, whose life, indeed, was recorded on endless strips of paper in incredible fables of wealth without work, of luxury without labor, and of fortunes made and remade at the flicker of a beady eye....So light your cigar with a hundred dollar bill, and G-

Charlie Mariano on baritone with Freddy Guerra's ensemble.

The 1951 annual concert was another elaborate affair. Twelve Schillinger House groups performed in all, including a new television revue segment featuring "Community Auditions" finalists and an accordion ensemble. *The Roaring Twenties*, another extended programmatic work, with scenario by George W. Clarke and individual movements each composed by a different student, was also featured. Clarke described the work as "a musical examination of a fabulous period in America's painful progress towards what is called Civilization." The "Panorama in Brass" segment featured a trumpet ensemble conducted by Supervisor of Brass Instruction Fred Berman. A former trumpeter with Paul Whiteman, Berman was a specialist in correcting embouchure problems. He remained with the school until his death in 1957. Among his students were Quincy Jones '51, Herb Pomeroy, and current Berklee President Lee Eliot Berk.

Clifford Brown records with Art Blakey.

Dave Brubeck on cover of *Time*.

"Sh-Boom" is first hit to cross over from R&B to pop charts.

Rosemary Clooney records "This Ole House."

January 14, 1954

Commonwealth of Massachusetts
Department of Education
Board of Collegiate Authority
200 Newbury St.
Boston, Mass.

Att: Mr. James Burke, Agent

Gentlemen:

As of January 20, 1954 we are changing the name of
our school from "Schillinger House" to "Berklee
School of Music".

Our courses, course content, fees and school policy
and staff will remain unchanged. Only the front and
back cover and title page of our school catalog will
be revised to read "Berklee School of Music" instead
of "Schillinger House".

We, therefore, request the approval of the board to
make this change in the name of the school.

Sincerely yours,

Lawrence Berk, Director
SCHILLINGER HOUSE

lb/kb

In less than 10 years, enrollment at Schillinger House had grown more than tenfold. Thanks to Berk's leadership, it had earned the respect and endorsement of national magazines and internationally prominent musicians. Alumni were found in many of the most popular and successful bands in the country.

Joseph Schillinger and his system still played an important role in the curriculum, but the school had evolved. Since the Schillinger House name no longer accurately reflected the distinctive vision and unique course of instruction offered at the school, in the early 1950s, Lawrence Berk began considering the idea of renaming the school.

"My father came home one evening and reported that Fred Berman had come into his office and said, 'Larry, I had a dream last night that the name of the school was changed to Berklee and named after Lee,'" President Lee Berk remembers. "'That's it!' he said, bestowing on me in an instant a unique distinction from the time I was 10 or 11 years old." In January 1954, Lawrence Berk fulfilled the dream of one of the school's premier faculty members and officially announced that Schillinger House was now the Berklee School of Music.

the SCORE

Berklee
SCHOOL OF MUSIC
Lawrence Berk DIRECTOR
FORMERLY schillinger house

BERKLEE SCHOOL OF MUSIC, BOSTON, MASSACHUSETTS.

MARCH, 1954

VOLUME 1, NO. 3

"DANSERO" LEE DANIELS
HITS NEW HIGH WITH
MUSICAL REVIEW CLASS

Musical Comedy Productions

Recognizing the need for a practical testing ground for the more elaborate routines learned in courses in Voice Production, Vocal Coaching and Dancing, this

SCHILLINGER HOUSE RENAMED
"BERKLEE SCHOOL OF MUSIC"

COURSES, TEACHING STAFF,
TEACHING METHOD ET AL.
REMAIN STATUS QUO

The recent change in the name of the School from Schillinger House to "BERKLEE SCHOOL OF MUSIC" was a move voted unanimously by the Faculty.

Chapter Two

Berklee School of Music
1955 – 1963

In the year that Lawrence Berk changed the name of his school from Schillinger House to Berklee School of Music, cold war tensions gripped the United States. Senator Joe McCarthy's witch hunt for Communist infiltrators in the United States government continued. The first hydrogen bomb test obliterated Bikini atoll in the South Pacific. And atom-bomb creator Robert Oppenheimer lost his security clearance.

But superpower politics were far from the minds of students at the Berklee School of Music. Under Lawrence Berk's continuing direction, new faculty, many of them successful jazz musicians who benefitted from Berk's unique curriculum, continued to build the stature of the Berklee School of Music as the first college-level school in the world where jazz was the basis of the curriculum. Nationally prominent bandleaders increasingly turned to the school for new talent, recruiting Berklee students right out of the classroom.

Berklee's reputation spread overseas, too. In the aftermath of World War II, jazz came to symbolize the political freedom and economic prosperity of the United States. Countries that were rebuilding their economies, and had the freedom to do so, wanted to emulate the United States, the leader of the victorious Allied powers. Countries that became closed to the West received news and heard American jazz on radio broadcasts by Voice of America. Aspiring jazz musicians from both sides of the Iron Curtain came to study at Berklee in increasing numbers.

Students Dave Matayabas (bass), Toshiko Akiyoshi (piano), Art Smith (saxophone), and faculty member Herb Pomeroy. Faculty like Pomeroy strengthened Berklee's reputation for excellence in jazz studies. Talented students from around the world, such as Akiyoshi, transformed Berklee into an international center for jazz education.

| **1955** Charlie Parker dies. | John Coltrane joins the Miles Davis Quintet. | Leonard Feather publishes first edition of *The Encyclopedia of Jazz.* | Horace Silver and Art Blakey form the Jazz Messangers. |

1955 Chuck Berry releases "Maybellene."   Bo Diddley releases self-titled debut single.   Little Richard releases "Tutti Frutti."

1955 RCA Mark I synthesizer developed.   Wurlitzer electric piano marketed.

Forty saxophonists greet Joe Viola as he returns from studies with classical saxophonist and educator Marcel Mule in Paris.

In September 1955, Joe Viola flew to Paris to study with Marcel Mule, the world's foremost classical saxophonist and a renowned educator and composer for the instrument. Viola first heard Mule on record with a saxophone quartet in 1937 and determined to study with him one day. Nearly 20 years later, at a demonstration of the new Selmer Mark VI saxophone, Maurice Selmer gave Mule's address in Paris to Viola. He wrote and Mule agreed to take him as a student. "He stressed practice more than anything else," Viola remembers. "That was probably the most important part of his philosophy." Viola's studies with Mule inspired him to found the Berklee Faculty Saxophone Quartet.

Lawrence Berk and 40 Berklee saxophone students, playing a medley of "La Marseilles" and "Stars and Stripes Forever" written especially for the occasion, greeted Viola upon his return as he stepped off a plane at Logan Airport.

1956 Horace Silver forms his own quintet.

Clifford Brown dies in auto accident.

1956 Elvis Presley charts 17 songs, including #1 single "Hound Dog."

James Brown releases "Please, Please, Please."

Little Richard releases "Long Tall Sally."

1956 Consumer stereo 2-track recordings for sale.

Boston Pops conductor Arthur Fiedler (left), Newport Jazz Festival impresario George Wein (middle), and Lawrence Berk hang *Down Beat* Hall of Fame plaques in the lobby of the Berklee School of Music.

Recognizing Berklee's preeminence in jazz education, *Down Beat* magazine selected it as the site of what many regarded as the first jazz museum in the country. To inaugurate the museum, the magazine sent reproductions of its Hall of Fame awards for public display at Berklee. In the mid-1950s, election to the *Down Beat* Hall of Fame was one of the few public honors jazz musicians received for outstanding artistic accomplishment. On display at Berklee, the plaques helped educate students and visitors about the important contributions of significant jazz figures. At 284 Newbury Street in the fall of 1955, Lawrence Berk, Boston Pops conductor Arthur Fiedler, and jazz impresario George Wein hung plaques for the first *Down Beat* Hall of Fame inductees—big band leaders Glenn Miller and Stan Kenton, and trumpeter Louis Armstrong. In later years, plaques commemorating Hall of Fame members Duke Ellington, Billie Holiday, and others were also displayed in the Berklee lobby.

47

Sonny Rollins records *Saxophone Collosus.*   Ellington triumphs at Newport.

Charles Mingus records *Pithecanthropus Erectus.*

Fats Domino releases "Blueberry Hill."   Doo-wop groups like the Platters, the Drifters, and the Penguins are popular.

The Herb Pomeroy big band in 1956.

In 1956, trumpeter Herb Pomeroy became a full-time Berklee faculty member. After attending Schillinger House, Pomeroy left the school in 1952 to pursue a career as a jazz trumpeter. After traveling wih the Stan Kenton and Lionel Hampton big bands, and playing with Charlie Parker and baritone saxophone great Serge Chaloff, he returned to Boston and joined the Berklee faculty. Around the same time, he also established and led a professional big band which included Berklee faculty and alumni. He would be among the premier jazz educators at Berklee for nearly four decades, until his retirement in 1995.

Pomeroy always worked with the most advanced students. "I was the guy who taught the best students and had fun with them," he says. His line writing courses were an incubator for some of the best jazz writing and arranging talent to emerge from Berklee. His upper-level ensembles would become proving grounds for Berklee's top students. His ability to rehearse a band, to hear and correct problem areas quickly, and maintain the group's interest and enthusiasm in the written material, inspired students for decades.

Of his students, Pomeroy says, "I'm really looking to see them be themselves, write jazz music as they feel it should be written. . . . As I put it in class: 'You have to be the meat and potatoes. What you're getting from me is a little flavoring, a little salt and pepper here and there. You've got to be true to yourself.'"

Herb Pomeroy, Toshiko Akiyoshi, and
Lawrence Berk, circa 1957.

Herb Pomeroy supervising a student quintet rehearsal, circa 1960. Students include trumpeter Dusko Goykovic '63, bassist Tony Teixeira '60, and tenor saxophonist Ted Casher '61.

1957 John Coltrane records *Blue Train* and joins Thelonious Monk's band.

Miles Davis and arranger Gil Evans record *Miles Ahead.*

Lambert, Hendricks, and Ross debut.

1957 Buddy Holly and the Crickets release "That'll Be the Day."

Ricky Nelson releases "Teenager's Romance" b/w "I'm Walkin."

Sam Cooke releases "You Send Me."

Elvis Presley releases "Jailhouse Rock" and "All Shook Up."

"I taught the best students and had fun with them."

Herb Pomeroy

Toshiko Akiyoshi (center) with
Max Roach (left) and Clifford Brown
in January 1956.

In the years after World War II, many students came to Berklee from countries outside the United States, but few had an impact as great as Toshiko Akiyoshi '59.

A Grammy-winning composer and big band leader, Toshiko Akiyoshi has been a trailblazer for women in an art form traditionally dominated by men. Classically trained, Akiyoshi was drawn to jazz at an early age, eventually abandoning medical school and developing into the foremost jazz pianist in Japan in the early 1950s. When Oscar Peterson heard her on a tour of Japan in 1953, he arranged a recording session for Norman Granz's Verve label, bringing her to the attention of American jazz audiences.

Shortly after the album came out, an army bass player named Tony Teixeira told her about a school in Boston where she could study jazz. (Teixeira later attended Berklee himself and taught at the school.) Akiyoshi wrote immediately to Lawrence Berk, "I do not know how to ask you, but please give me chance to study [sic]. I'll work very hard."

Lawrence Berk knew from her album and from talking with George Wein and others that Akiyoshi was a special talent. After a year of negotiation with the State Department and Japanese officials, Berk was able to offer her a full scholarship and mailed her a plane ticket to Boston. The Bud Powell-influenced pianist was instantly hailed as a major new talent.

After leaving Berklee, her greatest artistic triumphs came with the big band she led starting in 1966. The Toshiko Akiyoshi-Lew Tabackin Big Band consistently won critics and readers polls throughout the 1970s. Over the years, Toshiko Akiyoshi has made over 50 albums and garnered 11 Grammy nominations.

"There is no Japanese jazz, just as there is no American jazz," she said once in an interview. "If I play my music, it's mine, Toshiko's—not Japanese or American. It's an individual expression. Jazz is jazz no matter where it's played."

Louis Armstrong presents Toshiko Akiyoshi with a check to establish a scholarship in the name of his manager Joe Glaser (right), as Lawrence Berk watches. The scholarship endowed by Glaser in 1958 was among the first created by leaders in the jazz community to help deserving talent attend the school.

Toshiko Akiyoshi performing her *Jazz Suite for Orchestra* as a student in 1957.

"Jazz is my music. . . .

It brings out my experiences and dreams."

MONTAGE OF MODERN MUSIC
CONCERT PRESENTED BY STUDENTS OF
Berklee School of Music
AT
JOHN HANCOCK HALL
200 BERKLEY STREET, BOSTON
SATURDAY, APRIL 28, 1956, AT 2.00 P.M.
ENTIRE PROCEEDS TO STUDENT SCHOLARSHIP FUND
CONTRIBUTION $2.00

Bill Berry (standing, far right) solos on his original tune "A la Stan" with Herb Pomeroy's student ensemble.

Toshiko Akiyoshi, surrounded by trombonists under the direction of Berklee Supervisor of Brass Instruction John Coffey, covers her ears. This photo ran in several Boston papers prior to the 1956 "Montage of Modern Music."

The Toshiko Akiyoshi trio, with Dave Matayabas on bass and Les Harris on drums, at the 1956 annual concert.

The 1956 "Montage of Modern Music" featured some of the best jazz talent yet to attend the school. "What a brass section we had that year," Herb Pomeroy says of the jazz ensemble he coached in his first year as a full-time teacher. Of the band's five trumpeters, Paul Fontaine '56 and Everett Longstreth '56 both became Berklee instructors and members of Pomeroy's professional big band. Bill Berry '58 went on to play with Duke Ellington and formed his own big band on the West Coast in 1971. Bill Chase '58 formed the popular jazz-rock fusion band Chase in the early 1970s. Two outstanding drummers, Jake Hanna and Les Harris '56, alternated with the group. Hanna later joined Woody Herman's band, spent over a decade with the "Merv Griffin Show" studio orchestra, and recorded a string of albums for the Concord jazz label with musicians such as guitarists Herb Ellis and Joe Pass, and bassist Ray Brown. In 1968, Harris returned to teach at Berklee and headed the Tutorial Services Office, established to provide academic support to students from 1978 to 1993. He retired in 1995.

Another jazz highlight of the wide-ranging program was Toshiko Akiyoshi's trio with Dave Matayabas on bass and Harris on drums. The trio played two standards, "Laura" and "Just One of Those Things," and an Akiyoshi original, "39 West 52nd Street." A longtime Berklee employee, Matayabas taught bass at Berklee for many years and retired as director of payroll/personnel systems in 1995.

Joe Viola and his saxophone students presented "From Sax to Parker to Mule," a history of the saxophone that reflected Viola's interest in jazz and modern French classical composers. John Lydon (third from left), whom the students nicknamed "The White Owl," soloed in the style of Charlie Parker in the second part of the three-part suite.

53

1958 Miles Davis and Gil Evans record *Porgy and Bess.*	Paul Bley in Los Angeles with Ornette Coleman and Don Cherry.

| **1958** Elvis Presley's number comes up in the draft. | Chuck Berry releases "Johnny B. Goode." | Frank Sinatra releases *Frank Sinatra Sings for Only the Lonely.* |

1958 Pro 4 Channel, 1/2-inch tape recorders developed.

During the 1957 annual concert, Berklee students marked Duke Ellington's election to the *Down Beat* Hall of Fame by performing original tunes in the Ellington style and their own arrangements of Ellington's music. "We had some of the better students write music in the Ellington style, because we thought that would show more respect for the music than if we only played 'Take the A Train' or 'Mood Indigo'," Herb Pomeroy says. "He came over to the school and sat in with us at a rehearsal before the concert."

The idea for the Ellington tribute evolved into Pomeroy's Arranging in the Style of Duke Ellington course. In the course, students used what Pomeroy calls "Duke's philosophical approach to the band" to liberate their own style. In Pomeroy's view, the essence of Ellington's art is allowing his band members to fully express themselves. "The result is much richer than, say, five saxophones," he says. "It's five people."

Lawrence Berk continued to assemble a first-rate jazz faculty from among the progressive bebop musicians living in Boston. This group of music modernists, many of whom were former Schillinger House students, formed a musician-run organization called the Jazz Workshop, renting space for jam sessions and informal study. By the mid-1950s, workshop jam sessions were held at the Stables in Copley Square, where Herb Pomeroy led his big band twice a week, and other members led small combos on other nights. Many Jazz Workshop members joined the Berklee faculty, including pianist Ray Santisi, alto saxophonist Charlie Mariano, trumpeter Lennie Johnson, and bassist John Neves.

In 1957, Santisi and Mariano both started teaching at Berklee. In 1995, Santisi was still a faculty member, a cornerstone of jazz piano instruction at Berklee, and an active area professional performer. Mariano taught at Berklee until 1959, and then again between 1965 and 1969. He returned for a final year in 1975, after which he left to live and perform in Europe. In 1967, Mariano studied Indian music and the nathasvaram (a double reed instrument) in India and afterwards played an early form of jazz-world music fusion. He also initiated some of the first jazz-rock ensembles at Berklee.

Drummer Alan Dawson also started teaching at Berklee in 1957 and remained until 1975. Another acclaimed jazz master, Dawson was a member of the Lionel Hampton Big Band and the Boston-area big band of Sabby Lewis prior to his arrival at Berklee. He remained an active performer while on the faculty, working most notably with pianist Jaki Byard and saxophonist Booker Ervin '54 in the 1960s, and with pianist Dave Brubeck in the early 1970s.

Ray Santisi (at piano) and Charlie Mariano joined the faculty in 1957.

The Duke sits in during a rehearsal by Herb Pomeroy's student ensemble.

In 1957, the student Jazz Workshop Octet, coached by Ray Santisi, included (from left to right) Charles Bechler '65, piano; Bill Briggs '57, drums; Gene Cherico, bass; Jimmy Mosher, baritone saxophone; Roger DeLillo '57, trombone; Paul Fontaine, trumpet; Jack Parkhurst '57, alto saxophone; and Gordon Brisker '58, tenor saxophone.

At the 1957 "Montage of Modern Music" salute to Duke Ellington, Herb Pomeroy's student ensemble featured saxophonist Jimmy Mosher '58, who later played with Woody Herman and Buddy Rich, and who succeeded Joe Viola as chair of the Woodwind Department. James Progris '57, later assistant to the dean and an early film scoring teacher, played trombone. Bassist Gene Cherico '59, who also played in Toshiko Akiyoshi's trio at the concert, went on to play and record with Benny Goodman, Stan Getz, and Frank Sinatra.

With the addition of string players, Pomeroy's ensemble also played "Jazz Suite for Orchestra" by Akiyoshi. The four-part work was "an adventure in the world of orchestral composition in which she has turned her talents to the mysteries of instrumentation, arrangement, and musical expression in orchestral terms," the program book explained. The booklet concluded prophetically that this first large-scale work of hers "will unquestionably be followed by events of ever greater importance in the career of Toshiko Akiyoshi."

The concert jazz band that performed a tribute to Duke Ellington included bassist Gene Cherico and saxophonist Jimmy Mosher (far right, in front row).

| **1959** | Ornette Coleman records *The Shape of Jazz to Come.* | Miles Davis records *Kind of Blue.* | John Coltrane records *Giant Steps.* | Duke Ellington receives Pulitzer Prize for score to *Anatomy of a Murder.* | Lester Young and Billie Holiday both die. |
| | | **1959** | Alan Freed is convicted of taking payola. | Buddy Holly, Ritchie Valens, and the Big Bopper die in plane crash. | Berry Gordy forms Motown Records. | First Grammy Awards ceremony held. |

1960 *Ella in Berlin* released on *Verve*.	*Sarah Vaughan and Count Basie* released on Roulette.	Wes Montgomery records "While We're Young."	John Coltrane Quartet records "My Favorite Things."	Max Roach records *We Insist— Freedom Now!*
Ray Charles releases "What'd I Say."	**1960** Chubby Checker releases "The Twist."	Joan Baez, the Weavers, and John Lee Hooker appear at the Newport Folk Festival.	Bobby Darin's "Mack the Knife" wins Grammy Award.	Brenda Lee releases "I'm Sorry."
	1959 Vladimir Ussachevsky, Otto Luening, and Milton Babbit use RCA Mark II synthesizer.		**1960** Consumer stereo LP records for sale.	

For *Jazz in the Classroom*, volume 3, Joe Viola overdubbed up to six reed parts in classical and jazz works by composer and arranger Manny Albam.

In late 1957, Herb Pomeroy and Robert Share approached Lawrence Berk with the idea of starting a series of annual recordings of the best compositions written by Pomeroy's students each year. Accompanied by scores, the albums would serve as educational tools to demonstrate jazz writing and performance.

"Larry immediately saw the merit of it and okayed it," Pomeroy remembers. "It tied in nicely with what the school was about—teaching jazz music. At that point, I am not aware of anywhere else you could get a record and the corresponding score."

The first *Jazz in the Classroom* record started a Berklee institution that continued until 1980. Sent around the world, these sets of albums and scores provided important insight and understanding about the music and helped spread the word about the quality education available at Berklee.

Herb Pomeroy's ensemble was nicknamed the Recording Band for their annual forays into local recording studios to make *Jazz in the Classroom* LPs. "We did one per school year at the end of the fall semester in December," Pomeroy says. "Bob Share did the administrative work and took charge of the liner notes and album design. He also took a great deal of pleasure being the A&R man. I was in the studio, and he was in the booth, making any number of major decisions on which solos were the best, which take was the best."

The 1964 Recording Band. Back row (left to right): Jim Castaldi '66, Lin Biviano, Tony DiMaggio '66. Middle row (left to right): Charles Cassara '66, John McGill '66, Wes Nicholas '66, Alf Clausen '66 (standing). Front row (left to right): George Zonce '68, George Bookataub '66, Jerry Collins '65.

Robert Share in the control room.

Trumpeter Ray Kotwica joined the faculty in the fall of 1957. "I lived right next door to the school, at 286 Newbury," Kotwica says. "Joe Viola, who I knew from working at the Latin Quarter, introduced me to Larry." Kotwica later became chair of the Trumpet Department and was appointed distinguished chair when the larger Brass Department was created in 1989.

In the summer of 1958, Berklee offered its first summer intensive program, an eight-week course that began July 7. Beginning in the fall, Berklee established a joint program with the Boston Conservatory of Music through which Berklee students could earn a bachelor's degree. Dean Bobbitt had established relationships with the nearby conservatory, leading to the creation of a degree program that allowed Berklee students to take advantage of the educational strengths of each school. The joint undergraduate degree program was discontinued after Berklee secured degree-granting status in 1962.

Ray Kotwica.

| **1961** Eric Dolphy arranges Coltrane's *Africa/Brass* album; they tour Europe. | Billie Holiday is first woman in *Down Beat* Hall of Fame. | Duke Ellington scores *Paris Blues*. | Bill Evans trio with Scott LaFaro records at the Village Vanguard. |

| **1961** Ray Charles releases "Hit the Road, Jack." | The Primettes change their name to the Supremes and release "Buttered Popcorn." | Peter, Paul, and Mary debut. | The Marvelettes release "Please, Mr. Postman." | Phil Spector founds Phillies label. |

1961 Max Mathews develops a system for the digital synthesis of sound and music.

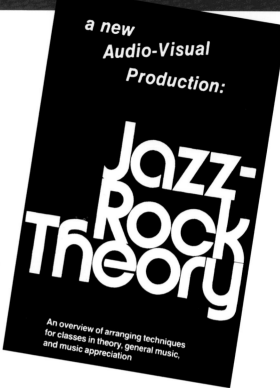

Creative Reading Studies for Saxophone
by Joseph Viola

BERKLEE SERIES—SAXOPHONE

THE TECHNIQUE OF THE SAXOPHONE

PART II

Chord Studies

JOSEPH VIOLA

a new Audio-Visual Production:

Jazz-Rock Theory

An overview of arranging techniques for classes in theory, general music, and music appreciation

the SCORE
Berklee school of music

VOLUME 10, NO. 5   BERKLEE SCHOOL OF MUSIC -- BOSTON, MASSACHUSETTS   MARCH, 1958

BERKLEE EXPANDS HORIZONS OF JAZZ EDUCATION WITH NEW DEGREE PROGRAM

STUDENTS MAY ENROLL FOR COURSES LEADING TO THE DEGREE OF BACHELOR OF MUSIC

"VOICE OF AMERICA" RECORDS AT BERKLEE FOR "MUSIC, USA"

(Standing, left to right) ARIF MARDIN, student-arranger from Istanbul, Turkey; winner of the Quincy Jones award — WILLIS CONOVER, producer of "Music, USA" for Voice of America — HERB POMEROY, Berklee instructor.

The cosmic news that Berklee School of Music has broadened the scope of jazz education to include a degree program has been greeted with rousing cheers by music students everywhere. In launching this, its latest satellite into orbit, Berklee has hurdled an obstacle which has long plagued those interested in a jazz education for it enables them to obtain a Bachelor of Music degree from a leading academic institution as well as a diploma from Berklee School of Music.

Aware that many students who were eager to attend Berklee were unable to do so because Berklee offered a diploma rather than a degree, directors at Berklee have tirelessly worked on this - what often seemed - insurmountable problem. In order to maintain Berklee's established instructional level with its curriculum geared to the efficient and thorough development of professional musicians, arrangers, and composers, it was considered impractical to revise established course material to include the academic studies of degree-granting institutions.

After a thorough study of the problem, however, Lawrence Berk, founder and director of Berklee School of Music, has arrived at a most happy solution: a plan of concurrent study in conjunction with one of New England's finest degree-granting institutions, which coordinates the Berklee curriculum with a full degree credit four year course. Upon completion of this combined course the student earns his Bachelor of Music degree together with his Certification from Berklee School.

(cont. page 2)

Record-Making News!

"JAZZ IN THE CLASSROOM" FOR THE FIRST TIME OFFERS JAZZ RECORDS AND SCORES FOR STUDY

Another milestone in the field of jazz education has been announced by Berklee School of Music, with its inspiring 12" LP - "Jazz in the Classroom", first of a series of educational LP's. Made up entirely of original compositions in the modern jazz idiom, it is conceived, created, arranged and performed by Berklee students and faculty, and is available with full scores of all arrangements for study and analysis.

"Jazz in the Classroom" offers a rare opportunity for musicians and music students to develop understanding of compositional and arranging techniques taught at Berklee. The techniques clearly outlined on the scores illustrate the most modern treatment of devices covered in Berklee classes such as combo and big band scoring, improvisation, polytonal voicings, thematic development and compositional form in jazz. Parts may be copied from scores for rehearsal and performance purposes.

Among the works represented are "Chaotic Suite", an extended form, jazz-influenced composition in three movements by Robert Freedman, and "Silhouette", a tender, slow-moving ballad by Toshiko Akiyoshi.

The recording ensembles were coached and conducted by Robert Freedman and Herb Pomeroy, both members of the instructional staff at Berklee.

You may order record and scores from convenient form enclosed.

Also in 1958, Berklee Press Publications was founded to publish student and faculty scores and instructional books written by faculty. Method books by William Curtis, Alan Dawson, and Joe Viola were some of the first published by Berklee Press. Later, books by John LaPorta, Andy McGhee, and William Leavitt were also published. Joe Viola's instruction book, among the most widely used music-study texts for saxophone, served as a model for instruction books for other instruments cowritten with other faculty.

Skip Beckwith '61, Michael Gibbs '63, Dizzy Sal Saldhana '63, Peter Spassoz '63, and Arif Mardin look over a score as they prepare for a Voice of America broadcast.

In the late 1950s, Berklee began to take on a decidedly international flavor. Knowledge of the jazz school in Boston spread around the world, in part through the relationship established with the United States Information Agency (USIA) and Voice of America—the government-funded radio network that broadcast news and American music to countries without a free press. Voice of America broadcasts, print media coverage of Berklee, educational materials distributed to nearly 50 countries, and the presence of Berklee alumni in jazz groups on USIA-sponsored international tours, all fueled the desire of jazz musicians around the world to study at Berklee.

While on a USIA-sponsored tour of the Middle East with the Dizzy Gillespie Orchestra in 1957, Berklee alumnus Quincy Jones was introduced to a young Turkish composer named Arif Mardin '61 by Voice of America official Tahir Sur. Looking over some of Mardin's arrangements, Jones was so impressed that when he returned to the United States, he recommended Mardin for a full scholarship to Berklee.

Mardin, of course, more than lived up to Jones' recommendation. The one-time radio arranger from Istanbul went on to become a senior vice president of Atlantic Studios. He produced the Bee Gees' Grammy-winning *Saturday Night Fever*, Judy Collins' "Send in the Clowns," Aretha Franklin's Grammy-winning album *Young, Gifted, and Black*, and coproduced Bette Midler's debut album *The Divine Miss M.*, with Barry Manilow. He delivered Berklee Commencement addresses in 1971, 1983, and received an honorary doctorate himself in 1985, the year his son Joe graduated from Berklee.

Arif Mardin, Lawrence Berk, and Tahir Sur.

Mardin remembers the close atmosphere at Berklee when he arrived in 1958. "The school was small—one townhouse, with a few hundred students. It was like a small family atmosphere," he said in an interview. "Larry Berk's office was downstairs; the late Bob Share was across the hall; Joe Viola was down the hall, teaching saxophone. It was a really wonderful family unit. Now, they have expanded it into something much bigger. But the warmth is still there."

Quincy Jones
55 West 52nd Street
New York 23, N. Y.
TEL. UNIVERSITY 2-2140

Hi Bob—

How's everything? — Hope the concert was swingin', I sure hated to miss it.

Here's the tape & necessary letters of recommendation for Arif MARDIN from Istanbul, Turkey who I think would be a wonderful candidate for a scholarship anywhere — You can contact him thru:

MR. TAHIR SUR
1906 K. STREET, N.W
WASH. 9, D.C.

My address in Paris:

Quincy Jones
% BARCLAY RECORDS
143 AV. de. NEUILLY
NEUILLY. SUR. SEINE
FRANCE—

Love to all & let me hear from you.—Bye.

Arif Mardin and Tahir Sur listen in the control room as bassist Skip Beckwith and guitarist Gabor Szabo '60 play for a Voice of America broadcast.

Herb Pomeroy rehearses the Radio Malaya Orchestra in 1962.

Lawrence Berk (left) and Ahmad Merican (standing, second from left) watch Herb Pomeroy rehearse a student band in jazz arrangements of Malayan folk songs.

In 1959, a Berklee group appeared on "Jazz with Father O'Connor" on WGBH-TV in a program of Malayan music played in a jazz style. Shown here in the WGBH studio are (from left to right): student Gabor Szabo, faculty guitar instructor Chet Kruley, faculty drum instructor Alan Dawson, Father Norman O'Connor, Ahmad Merican, student John Neves, Administrator Robert Share, WGBH assistant producer James Healy, and faculty saxophonist Charlie Mariano.

In August 1958, Malayan radio official Ahmad Merican '59 visited Berklee as part of an international radio-TV seminar group sponsored by the State Department. He asked Berklee students to write jazz arrangements of Malayan folk tunes for the country's Independence Day celebration. Malaya achieved independence from Great Britain in 1957. In 1963 it became a territory of Malaysia.

While attending Berklee, Merican wanted to develop his ear so he could transcribe his country's folk music and preserve it. Faculty member William Curtis created a course of study for him that became the basis for Berklee's Ear Training classes. "I found a quick way to establish where home base was in each key and identify each note of the scale. It was much quicker to learn than solfege," Curtis says. "Within the year he could use his ear to identify what he heard."

Several years later, in 1962, Merican arranged through the USIA for Herb Pomeroy to train the Radio Malaya Orchestra in Kuala Lumpur. The lead trumpet player, Johari Salleh '67, came to Berklee on a scholarship on Pomeroy's recommendation. Salleh later became the leader of the Malaysian Television Orchestra.

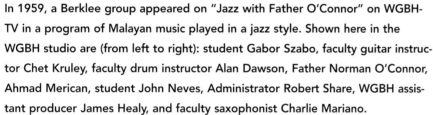

1962	Nancy Wilson records with Cannonball Adderley Quintet.	Stan Getz records Antonio Carlos Jobim's "Girl From Ipanema."	Sonny Rollins returns from retirement with *The Bridge*.	
1962 Bob Dylan debuts with *Bob Dylan*.	Beach Boys release "Surfin' Safari."	Booker T and the MGs release "Green Onions."	Ray Charles releases "I Can't Stop Lovin' You."	Neil Sedaka scores a #1 hit with "Breaking Up Is Hard to Do."
		1962 Consumer stereo 1/4-track records for sale.		

The 1962 Berklee International Jazz Octet included: trumpeter Dusko Goykovich from Yugoslavia; Mike Gibbs from Rhodesia; Peter Spassov from Yugoslavia; bassist Graham Collier from England; baritone saxophonist Jack Stevens from the United States; pianist Dizzy Sal Saldhana from India; tenor saxophonist Conrado Gregorio from Hong Kong; and alto saxophonist Heinz Bigler from Switzerland.

Mike Gibbs.

Formed in 1959, the Berklee International Jazz Sextet drew from the best of the school's international students. The band played jazz settings of music from student's respective countries as well as standard jazz repertory.

Trombonist and composer Michael Gibbs was a founding member of the International Jazz Sextet. After graduating from Berklee, he became a pioneer of jazz-rock fusion and a brilliant orchestrator. He returned to Berklee in the 1970s as an artist-in-residence, conducting student ensembles in his innovative compositions.

Gibbs arrived in Boston from Rhodesia (now Zimbabwe) in January 1959. As Gary Burton tells the story, "Mike had flown here and arrived at five in the morning. He took a cab to the school, but of course no one was there. There were two doors to the school and a foyer in between, so he got into the vestibule and stood in there with his trombone and suitcase in the cold. And around 7:30, the door opens up and it's Larry Berk arriving to open the school. That was his first greeting."

1963 John Coltrane records *Impressions* live at Village Vanguard.	Charles Mingus records *Black Saint and the Sinner Lady*.	Bill Evans records *Conversations With Myself*, multitrack recording improvisation.	Herbie Hancock joins Miles Davis Quintet.	Lee Morgan records *The Sidewinder*.
	1963 Starting with "Please Please Me," the Beatles release a string of #1 hits in the U.K.		Little Stevie Wonder releases "Fingertips, Part 2."	The Angels release "My Boyfriend's Back."

In 1959, the Berklee International Sextet included (from left to right): saxophonists Ted Casher and Dick Johnson, both from the Boston area; trombonist Mike Gibbs from Rhodesia; drummer Peter Spassov from Yugoslavia; bassist Skip Beckwith from Canada; and guitarist Gabor Szabo from Hungary.

William Maloof, founding chair of
the Composition Department.

Student vibraphonist Gary Burton leads his quartet,
with Steve Marcus on tenor, Jay Leonhart on bass,
and Tommy Check on drums, in concert at Newton
High School in April 1961.

Among the entering freshmen in the fall of 1960, was a young vibraphonist from Indiana, Gary Burton. "I came to Berklee right from high school, but probably half the students were older guys on the GI Bill," Burton says. "There was a lot of energy and vitality at the school because we all knew each other and you'd end up working gigs with the teachers on the weekends. The number-one favorite band in jazz was the Miles Davis group with Wynton Kelly, Cannonball Adderley, and John Coltrane. The Bill Evans trios were also big at the time. In those days, the biggest number of instruments were the drums. There were 50 drummers and maybe half a dozen of each other instrument. I don't remember any guitar players at the time."

Burton led a student quartet that substituted for Herb Pomeroy's combo at the Stables and played area concerts. Besides Burton, members of the band included drummer Tommy Check '61 and tenor saxophonist Steve Marcus '61, who later recorded on Burton's 1966 *Country Roads* album, and worked with Stan Kenton, Herbie Mann, and Larry Coryell. The bassist Jay Leonhart '61 later played with Lee Konitz, Gerry Mulligan, and others, and recorded several albums of his own songs.

William Maloof began teaching at Berklee in 1961 and later became the founding chair of the Composition Department. Through his courses, students learned traditional classical composing and conducting skills that broadened their studies of jazz and contemporary music. He retired in 1989.

Current Film Scoring Department Chair Don Wilkins '70, a former student of Maloof's, says, "It enhances a writer to know how to compose in a traditional setting, to understand the fundamentals of part writing, going back to sixteenth century techniques and right up to the twentieth century. That knowledge is of value to any kind of writer, because if you have those tools you've got more to work with."

In April 1969, John LaPorta conducted a big band tribute to his friend, composer/arranger and bandleader Johnny Richards, who died in late 1968. The program featured music by LaPorta written in honor of Richards and many of Richards' scores for Stan Kenton.

John LaPorta arrived to begin teaching at Berklee in time for the 1962 intensive summer semester, which had grown from one six-week offering into two six-week courses, one 12-week, and a one-week Music Educators Clinic.

A founding member of the Jazz Composers' Workshop in New York with Charles Mingus and others, reed player and composer LaPorta also played with Lennie Tristano and Woody Herman. He met Robert Share at a Stan Kenton Stage Band Clinic in the summer of 1961, and Share asked him to visit Berklee and see if he would like to teach there. "I visited that fall," LaPorta says, "and started the next summer."

LaPorta, creator and founding chair of the Instrumental Performance Department (precursor to the Performance Studies Department), had a far-reaching impact on Berklee. "Within three years, John was something of an icon and running all sorts of programs," current Professional Performance Division Chair Larry Monroe '70 recounts. "His attitude has always been 'If you can play a little, we can fit you in and make you play better.' John knew how to take a bunch of kids who had music in them and go forward with that. That was a breakthrough for the school. John was magnificent with lower-level kids. He could get music out of three stones and a corn cob."

"I think I've been able to bring out the unknown talents in students," says LaPorta, who retired in 1985. "I think as a teacher I should be concerned about hidden talents, not obvious ones. We're supposed to help people grow and become whatever they can."

Founding Chair of the Guitar Department Jack Peterson (left) teaches a private lesson.

In the early 1960s, guitar players had nowhere to learn music fundamentals and performance techniques, since traditional music conservatories did not recognize guitar as a principal instrument. Berklee responded to this educational need with the first college-level program providing guitarists with the opportunity to study jazz and contemporary music. On John LaPorta's recommendation, a North Texas State Teachers College graduate named Jack Peterson was hired in 1962 to create and build a guitar department.

Peterson began with just nine students and built the foundation of today's Guitar Department, the largest instrumental department at Berklee. He left after three years to pursue a studio career and eventually returned to teaching.

"I've always encouraged students to play what they love," he said at a 1993 clinic at Berklee. "But along with it they've got to learn their instrument. They have to know how to handle it."

Nonprofit Tag To Aid Berklee

THE CHRISTIAN SCIENCE MONITOR

FRIDAY, DECEMBER 29, 1961

For several years, Lawrence Berk had struggled with the question of how to ensure the school's continued success. He consulted with several close associates, and decided to put the school on a nonprofit basis. He hoped this would give Berklee "stability, longevity, and acceptance for its special kind of educational processes." In January 1962, Lawrence Berk transformed his burgeoning music school into a nonprofit institution under an independent Board of Trustees. And in 1963, he announced that the class entering that year would be the first to qualify for a bachelor's degree from the Berklee School of Music.

---

the SCORE
Berklee school of music

Vol. 12 No. 8   BERKLEE SCHOOL OF MUSIC -- BOSTON, MASSACHUSETTS   1964

Guidance Counselors Endorse

Evaluation Clinic - Highlight of Summer Program

Just as one tests the ocean with his big toe to see if it's warm enough for the big plunge, Berklee's remarkable 6-Week Summer Evaluation Clinic tests the young student for his degree of potential for a career in the world of music.

Thus, considerable time, money and effort are properly channeled for if the student demonstrates enough talent and aptitude for a career, he is encourage to pursue his goals; if, on the other hand, he is lacking in ability and interest, these all-important facts will be obvious before the student embarks on a costly and time-consuming college program. At the end of the clinic, parent and high school guidance counselor receive a detailed evaluation report prepared by the Berklee Dean's Office. Whim and starry-eyed dreams are sifted from genuine talent and potential success.

This summer, Berklee's 6-Week Evaluation Clinics start on June 8 and July 20.

In addition to the 6-Week Evaluation Clinics, Berklee continues to offer its intensive 12-Week Summer Course which earns the student credit for one full semester. Starting date for the 12-Week Course is June 8.

Regular faculty members staff both programs and the curriculum includes theory, arranging, modern chord progression, ear training, stage band, private instrumental instruction, improvisation, ensemble, jazz workshop.

Inquiries on either program will be promptly answered. Fill out enclosed card for further information.

Goody from Woody

Herman Gives Berklee A Big Bouquet in New York Times Interview

In a recent "New York Times" interview, Woody Herman was asked by John S. Wilson how he kept finding talent for his band.

"One of them recommends another," Woody stated. "Right now I've found a fountain of talent in New England. Most of them have been to the Berklee School of Music in Boston which seems to be turning out more good musicians than any of the other schools."

a matter of degree
Now Berklee Offers Its Own Degree Program
Plus Its Famous Professional Diploma Course

What began five years ago as a major experiment in the field of American music education has flourished into an unprecedented program of working reality. So successful has been the degree program which was inaugurated at that time, that it has become a vital factor in the curriculum, and as of this fall is BERKLEE-CONCEIVED AND ADMINISTERED THROUGHOUT!

Thus, in a brief time by educational standards, Berklee is the only college in the world offering a degree which includes emphasis on American music, a fact which is viewed with considerable pride by all those who have worked so diligently to attain this goal.

In making the momentous announcement, Lawrence Berk, director, stated that all of the educational music techniques for which Berklee is famous, will remain in effect, and that the new program will round out and supplement the established curriculum.

New faculty members will be added to the staff for the express purpose of teaching academic courses and more diversified music courses. Mr. Berk emphasizes the work "added," stressing that the basic music curriculum which has proven so successful in the past will remain essentially the same.

Delighted and proud as they are of the new Degree Program, both Mr. Berk and Robert Share, administrator, will also continue to develop and augment the strikingly successful Professional Diploma Course for those whose career interests are concerned with professional music, for as Mr. Berk stresses, "Berklee is still and always will be a specialist training institution."

With its continued growth in all areas, Berklee maintains its role as one of the world's truly vital educational forces in the field of American music.

Stan Kenton drops in on rehearsal session of Berklee students in an informal visit. A frequent visitor to the famous school, Stan has recently been named to Berklee's National Advisory committee.

Benny Golson visits with Berklee students on a recent tour of the school. Benny's compositions inspired "Jazz in the Classroom, Vol. V.," scores and LP arranged and performed by Berklee students.

...rence Berk, a graduate of Massachusetts Institute of Technology and head of the mechanical design section on radar receivers at Raytheon Company, taught a few students in music theory and arranging just to keep up his interest in music.

He had worked his way through college playing piano and arranging for a local Boston dance band. Later, he went to New York, where he studied with Joseph Schillinger, composer, natural scientist, and teacher, who developed a special mathematical system of musical composition... Schillinger...

...Sponsored by the Peña de Jazz of Montevideo, the Gary Burton Quartet from Berklee will travel around participating in jazz concerts, conferences, debates, and jam sessions.

The group, consisting of Gary Burton, vibraphone; Dan Martin, drums; Don Jones, bass; and Chris Swansen, valve trombone, will begin their tour Jan. 31 in Punta del Este and end in Montevedeo Feb. 6.

The Berklee group will represent the United States, while other groups will represent Argentina, Chile, Brazil, and Uruguay.

Educational...

Chapter Three

Berklee School of Music
1964 – 1970

As Berklee bestowed its first bachelor's degrees on the class of 1966, the school faced a student population explosion and a major change in popular music. A newer, larger home for Berklee at 1140 Boylston Street opened in 1966 to accommodate current enrollment and anticipated growth. In the years immediately preceeding the school's relocation and its first awarding of college degrees, Berklee added new faculty who strengthened its traditional course offerings and the jazz curriculum for which it was best known. By the end of the decade, faculty began to create the first college-level courses ever offered in rock and pop music. With the ascendancy of rock and roll, the Guitar Department, which offered the first opportunity for guitarists to receive a college-level music education, began to draw growing numbers of students to the school. As Berklee celebrated its 25th anniversary in 1970, Lawrence Berk could survey a dramatically larger institution that was successfully changing with the times, but which still preserved its core strengths in jazz performance, composition, and arranging.

Berklee
school of music

A degree granting institution offering concentration in American music.

Degree Program majors in

- Music Education
- Composition
- Performance

Diploma Program majors in

- Arranging & Composition
- Performance

Summer Program

- Evaluation clinic for high school undergraduates
- Full credit 12 week course

All majors include instruction in modern harmony, arranging improvisation, ensemble.

For information & catalog write to:

1964 John Coltrane Quartet records *A Love Supreme.*

Don Ellis forms his first big band.

Horace Silver records *Song for My Father.*

1964 The Beatles lead the "British Invasion" with three gold albums.

Mary Wells releases "My Guy."

The Temptations release "The Way You Do the Things You Do."

The Righteous Brothers release "You've Lost That Loving Feeling."

1964 Robert A. Moog develops the Voltage-Controlled Oscillator and Voltage-Controlled Amplifier of his modular Moog synthesizer.

The first class to earn a bachelor of music degree from the Berklee School of Music enters New England Life Hall for graduation ceremonies in May 1966.

Berklee continued to build its growing Composition Department with the addition of John Bavicchi to the faculty in 1964. Over the years, he worked closely with Composition Department Chair William Maloof in developing the traditional music curriculum at Berklee. Bavicchi not only taught composition, but music history and conducting as well. An active composer with over 100 works, he had won 28 ASCAP Awards for his compositions since the award was instituted in 1960. He retired in 1995.

John Bavicchi.

Phil Wilson (right) with Woody Herman (center) and Louis Armstrong at the Grammy Awards in New York in 1964. Andy McGhee, who began teaching at Berklee in 1966, is in the saxophone section.

Phil Wilson in the trombone section of the Woody Herman Swinging Herd during a rehearsal at Berklee.

Berklee significantly strengthened its jazz curriculum with the addition of trombonist Phil Wilson. Founding chair of the Trombone Department, Wilson started teaching at Berklee in 1965, after working with the Dorsey Brothers and Woody Herman. A Grammy Award nominee for his arrangement of "Mercy, Mercy, Mercy" (which was composed by Joe Zawinul '59) for the Buddy Rich Big Band, Wilson helped create a unique program at Berklee for the study of contemporary music for trombone. In addition, his student ensemble, the Dues Band (later called the Rainbow Band) became one of the most popular and prestigious student ensembles at Berklee. Concerts by the Dues Band were among the first at Berklee to include rock and funk along with jazz. "Teaching is a two-way street for me," Wilson says. "As you give, so do you receive. I love to play and I always have, and I think a student sees that in me and is likely to give back."

William Leavitt, shortly after leaving Schillinger House.

Jack Peterson left Berklee in 1965, and Robert Share asked William Leavitt, an alumnus of Schillinger House and a busy Boston-area studio and theater musician, to take over the Guitar Department. Leavitt agreed to fill in for a year until a new chair could be hired. He stayed until his death in 1990.

Leavitt, only the third guitarist to attend Schillinger House, had a dramatic and far-reaching impact on guitar pedagogy. "Rather than being primarily a performer, Bill was primarily an arranger and composer," says current Associate Dean of Faculty Ronald Bentley, a former student of Leavitt's. "He took the discipline he learned as a writer and applied it to teaching guitar. He gave some structure to learning guitar and no one had ever done that before him. In the process, he legitimized the guitar." Leavitt used his arranging skills in the 355 arrangements he wrote for guitar ensembles. Many of them are still used today as teaching exercises. The 10 instruction books Leavitt wrote are considered classics. He "wrote the bible for guitarists, the guide to learning to play it in real musical terms," says Bentley.

As a student, Leavitt wrote "My Baby's Coming Home," a hit for Les Paul and Mary Ford. One of his co-authors, Sherm Feller, is best remembered as the Boston Red Sox's Fenway Park announcer.

Leavitt thought Red Sox pitcher Jim Lonborg "has potential"—as a guitarist—after his first private lesson. Shortstop Rico Petrocelli, who was studying percusssion and vibraphone with Berklee faculty member Lou Magnano, recommended Berklee to Lonborg. Petrocelli claimed practicing limbered up his arms and helped him on the field.

Guitar Department Chair William Leavitt (far left) joins a faculty all-star group with (from left to right) Ray Santisi, John LaPorta, Charlie Mariano, Phil Wilson, Alan Dawson, Herb Pomeroy, and William Curtis.

William Leavitt conducts an early guitar ensemble.

In a 1983 interview with *Guitar Player* magazine, Leavitt explained his teaching philosophy. "I'd like to be able to prepare every student to support himself or herself in the music world," he said. At Berklee, "we try to give them a picture of what it's really like in the professional world, and attempt to get them to develop abilities that will allow them to handle the problems and situations they're going to have to deal with."

79

Sadao Watanabe with the Recording Band.

Sadao Watanabe.

Berklee bolstered its status as an international center of jazz education throughout the 1960s. Japanese saxophonist Sadao Watanabe '65 was encouraged to attend Berklee by alumna Toshiko Akiyoshi, in whose quartet he played before she came to the United States. In a 1991 interview in *Berklee today*, Watanabe recalled arriving in 1962 with little more than his instruments, a blanket, and a frying pan. He left Berklee in 1965 to play with vibraphonist Gary McFarland '60, a job for which Herb Pomeroy recommended him. After returning to Tokyo in 1966, he was appointed head of the new Yamaha Institute of Popular Music. In 1976, he was the first jazz musician to receive the Grand Prix Award from the Japanese government's cultural agency. By 1995, Watanabe had made over 50 albums reflecting his eclectic tastes from jazz-rock fusion to bossa nova to straight-ahead jazz.

Sadao Watanabe (center) and Charlie Mariano (left) at a jam session in Japan.

Robert Share (far right) stands next to Sadao Watanabe, circa 1962. Faculty members (seated, from left to right) are John LaPorta, Joe Viola, and Pat Principe.

1965	John Coltrane records *Ascension*.	Duke Ellington debuts first sacred jazz concert in San Francisco.	Thad Jones and Mel Lewis form a big band.	Herbie Hancock records *Maiden Voyage*.	Sun Ra records *The Magic City*.
1965	The Byrds release first folk-rock hit "Mr. Tambourine Man."	Bob Dylan releases his first electric folk-rock album *Bringing It All Back Home*.	The Rolling Stones release "Satisfaction."	Lou Reed forms Velvet Underground.	
				1965 Commercial production of 8-track, 1-inch tape recorders.	Distortion "fuzz boxes" for guitars are marketed.

The Class of 1966. First row (from left to right): Michael Rendish, Alan Marino, Steven Gould (B.M. in Composition), Alf Clausen, Anthony DiMaggio, Nicholas Aksionczyk (Diploma in Arranging and Composition). Second row: Richard Milgram, John McGill, John Julian, James Castaldi, Charles Cassara, George Bookataub. Third row: unidentified, unidentified, Gerald Reber, Ted Pease, William Moulton, Joseph Miller (last two rows all earned a B.M. in Music Education).

Presiding over the graduation exercises were (from left to right) Richard Bobbitt, Dean; Robert Share, Administrator; James Progris, Assistant Dean; William Curtis, Registrar; Lawrence Berk, President; and Professor Roland Nadeau, critic and Chair of the Northeastern University Music Department, who delivered the Commencement address.

The first Berklee Trombone Ensemble, including trombonist Sam Burtis '66 (fifth from left) and drummer John Betsch '66 (partially hidden), performs at the 1966 Commencement concert.

Professor William Maloof conducts the Concert Band at the 1966 Commencement concert. Among the band members are Alf Clausen (third French horn player from left) and Ernie Watts, playing piccolo.

On May 28, 1966, Berklee awarded its first bachelor of music degrees to a graduating class. Thirteen students received bachelor's degrees in music education and three in composition. Three students received diplomas in arranging and composition.

The Commencement concert that immediately followed the baccalaureate ceremony featured the Berklee Trombone Ensemble, among other student ensembles. Professor of Trombone Phil Wilson established the ensemble during his first year at the school. "Trombone Ensemble was an attempt to get people to look at the trombone in a new way," Wilson says. "It's a much more versatile instrument than people allow. They think of the circus, they think of Wagner, and a few other things. But the traditional literature for the trombone is lacking. As a composer, I was very eager to open the thinking of trombonists. And when you look at the results, what our graduates have done for the instrument, I think we succeeded."

Another ensemble heard during the concert, William Maloof's student concert orchestra, featured two students who later achieved fame. Saxophonist Ernie Watts left Berklee in 1966 to join Woody Herman's band and went on to a jazz and studio career in Los Angeles, where he played with Doc Severinsen's "Tonight Show" Orchestra, Frank Zappa, and Charlie Haden's Quartet West. Composer Alf Clausen also went to Hollywood, where he has scored many popular TV shows, including "Moonlighting" and "The Simpsons."

Berklee
School of Music

presents

A Concert of
instrumental music

New England Life Hall
225 Clarendon St. Boston
Saturday afternoon May 28th
2:00 pm

Hotel Bostonian Boston, Mass.

Berklee had finally run out of room on Newbury Street, so when the Hotel Bostonian came up for sale in 1965, Lawrence Berk saw the perfect opportunity for his school to expand into new and larger quarters. Berklee would need the space; between 1966, when the school moved into its new building, and 1969, enrollment increased from 582 to 912.

Announcing
MODERN JAZZ EVERY NITE
IN THE
Burgundy Room - Hotel Bostonian
OPENING WEDNESDAY, DECEMBER 27, 1950
Nick Jerret presents
CHARLIE MARIANO
Boston's Amazing Altoist
PLUS
SAUL WEISMAN, Drums   FRANK VACCARO, Bass
SONNY TRUETT, Piano   VITO PAUL, Piano
PLUS
Many Others for Future Presentation
HOTEL BOSTONIAN   1138 BOYLSTON STREET
KEnmore 6-5617

Lawrence Berk inspects the work in progress at 1140 Boylston Street.

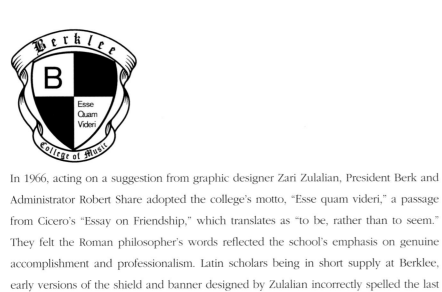

Berklee
B
Esse
Quam
Videri
College of Music

84

In 1966, acting on a suggestion from graphic designer Zari Zulalian, President Berk and Administrator Robert Share adopted the college's motto, "Esse quam videri," a passage from Cicero's "Essay on Friendship," which translates as "to be, rather than to seem." They felt the Roman philosopher's words reflected the school's emphasis on genuine accomplishment and professionalism. Latin scholars being in short supply at Berklee, early versions of the shield and banner designed by Zulalian incorrectly spelled the last word as "videre," but the typographical error was soon corrected.

A worker removes a letter from the marquee of the Hotel Bostonian during renovations to create the new Berklee School of Music.

At the open house to celebrate Berklee's new location, inventor Harold Rhodes (right) tries one of 24 Fender Rhodes electric pianos Berklee acquired for an electronic keyboard lab. William Maloof (left) listens through headphones.

to our visitors

It is indeed a pleasure for us to welcome you here today for the official opening of our new facilities, specially-designed to give maximum effect to our continuing innovations in methods of teaching and learning.

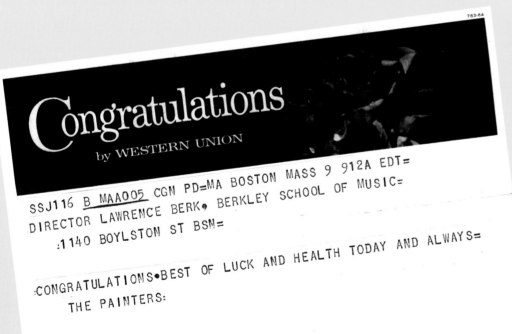

Congratulations
by WESTERN UNION

SSJ116 B MAAOO5 CGN PD=MA BOSTON MASS 9 912A EDT=
DIRECTOR LAWRENCE BERK. BERKLEY SCHOOL OF MUSIC=
:1140 BOYLSTON ST BSN=

:CONGRATULATIONS.BEST OF LUCK AND HEALTH TODAY AND ALWAYS=
THE PAINTERS:

The new facilities at 1140 Boylston Street officially opened in the fall of 1966. Over 500 visitors attended the grand opening of the new Berklee School of Music facilities on September 9. Extensive renovations had transformed the old hotel where faculty members such as Dean Earl and Charlie Mariano had once played. Renovations split the building's interior vertically. On one side former hotel rooms served as dormitory space. The other side contained classrooms, practice rooms, and offices. The library and tape deck facilities were located on the sixth floor. The third floor contained an electronic piano room, equipped with 24 electric pianos for group functional keyboard instruction, monitored through headphones by a faculty member. A recital hall and student lounge were located on the ground floor. Ensemble rooms, the bookstore, and the Berklee Press print shop were found on the basement level.

Board of Trustee members Willis Conover, Herbert Baer, James Zafris, Jr., and Richard Rhodes Wilton at a Commencement buffet.

In September 1966, Berklee established its first Board of Trustees. Gregory Larkin, for many years an advisor to Lawrence Berk on veterans' affairs, was elected the first chair. In 1970, Larkin temporarily left the board to establish Berklee's first Office of Financial Aid, but returned in 1975 and served for another ten years. Larkin was succeeded as director of financial aid by Joe Ferrari, who served from 1975 to 1990, when Pam Gilligan became director.

Other members of the board included: Willis Conover, the jazz voice of Voice of America; jazz priest Reverend Norman O'Connor; and bankers Richard Wilton and James G. Zafris, Jr. Zafris was later chair of the Board of Trustees.

In 1969, the Board of Trustees elected several more members. Alumni Quincy Jones, who later became a member of the Board of Overseers, and Arif Mardin both joined the board at the June meeting. Investment consultant Alan Tucker, banker Calvin Perry, and newspaper publisher William Plante, also became members.

Founding Chair of the Board of Trustees Gregory Larkin (left) and Lawrence Berk.

1966 Cecil Taylor records *Unit Structures*.	Keith Jarrett performs with the Charles Lloyd Quartet.	Buddy Rich forms big band.	Duke Ellington records *Far East Suite*.
1966 The Beach Boys release "Good Vibrations."	Simon and Garfunkel have a #1 hit with "Sounds of Silence."	The Monkees make TV debut and chart #1 hit "Last Train to Clarksville."	The Rascals have their first #1 hit "Good Lovin'."	Three Beatles' albums go gold: *Rubber Soul, Revolver, Yesterday and Today.*
		1966 Psychedelic clubs popularize light shows.		

Alma Berk (seated, center) and the faculty wives.

Mrs. Berk converses with bassist Jiri (George) Mraz '70 at the first Sherry Hour in 1969. The annual Sherry Hour for entering international students continued through 1993.

Charlie Mariano (right) and Mrs. Berk with Abraham Laboriel, Sr., '72 at the 1969 Sherry Hour.

Alma Berk became director of public information in 1966, and would manage Berklee media relations until her retirement in 1994. Prior to that, she had managed the former Newton Branch of the Berklee School of Music. As the wife of Lawrence Berk, she was familiar with Berklee since its founding, and had a keen sense of the news value of Berklee activities. In her capacity as director of public information, she provided information to major Boston media outlets, national magazines, and literally thousands of newspapers around the world.

The original Berklee Faculty Saxophone Quartet (from left to right): Joe Viola, John LaPorta, Richard Wright '65, and Rod Ferland '65.

In 1966, Joe Viola, John LaPorta, Richard Wright, and Rod Ferland formed the Berklee Faculty Saxophone Quartet. The quartet's repertoire included the French classical repertoire for saxophone quartet, arrangements of jazz and classical works, and compositions by faculty members such as John Bavicchi, William Maloof, and Jeronimas Kacinskas. Quartet members, including LaPorta and Gary Anderson '69, also contributed pieces.

The Berklee Faculty Saxophone Quartet in 1970 (from left to right): Joe Viola, John LaPorta, Gary Anderson, and Harry Drabkin '69.

Andy McGhee solos with the Lionel Hampton band. Sammy Davis, Jr., (left) plays the drums.

Andy McGhee with Red Skelton.

Andy McGhee with Woody Herman.

The 1966 arrival of saxophonist Andy McGhee added another strong jazz talent to the faculty. His broad professional experience included work with Woody Herman, Lionel Hampton, Sammy Davis, Jr., Tony Bennett, and comedian Red Skelton. His musical credentials, coupled with a solid educational background, made him a valuable addition to the school.

Fred Buda conducts the percussion ensemble at the 1967 Commencement concert.

1967 The Beatles release *Sgt. Pepper's Lonely Hearts Club Band.*

Eric Clapton, Jack Bruce, and Ginger Baker form Cream.

Aretha Franklin signs with Atlantic Records.

The Doors perform "Light My Fire" on "The Ed Sullivan Show."

The Class of 1967. John Abercrombie is seated second in the front row.

Andy McGhee (right) with a student ensemble featuring Richie Cole on alto saxophone and Hal Grossman on trumpet.

Nineteen students received degrees and three received diplomas in the class of 1967, the first to graduate after Berklee relocated to 1140 Boylston Street. Among those to earn a diploma was guitarist John Abercrombie. One of the most in-demand guitarists of his generation, Abercrombie recorded extensively on the ECM label beginning in 1974, most notably as a member of the cooperative Gateway Trio with Dave Holland and Jack DeJohnette; as the leader of a quartet with Richie Beirach, George Mraz, and Peter Donald between 1978 and 1981; and as the leader of a trio with organist Dan Wall.

A small jazz ensemble led by faculty member Andy McGhee was one of several student ensembles to perform at the Commencement concert. It featured student alto saxophonist Richie Cole '67 and student trumpeter Hal Grossman '69. Two years after this concert, Cole left Berklee to play with drummer Buddy Rich. He later played with jazz vocalist Eddie

Jefferson, trumpeter Red Rodney, and led his own groups, including Alto Madness. Hal Grossman, brother of saxophonist Steve Grossman, taught at Berklee from 1969 to 1989.

Student drummers and percussionists in an ensemble directed by faculty percussionist Fred Buda also played at the 1967 Commencement concert. Student percussion virtuoso Stomu Yamash'ta, provided a concert highlight. Yamash'ta, who had appeared with the Tokyo Symphony before coming to Berklee, later recorded works by classical composers Hans Werner Henze and Peter Maxwell Davies, and in the 1970s led the Red Buddha Theater, an innovative band that drew on classical, rock, traditional Japanese, and jazz influences.

The Commencement speaker was Dr. Abraham Schwadron, Chair of the Rhode Island College Music Department.

1967 Miles Davis quintet records *Nefertiti.*   John Coltrane dies.   Toshiko Akiyoshi forms her first big band.

Steve Winwood leaves the Spencer Davis Group to form Traffic.   *Hair,* "an American tribal love-rock musical," opens off-Broadway.   Jimi Hendrix releases *Are You Experienced?*

Jeronimas Kacinskas.

Another mainstay of the Composition Department, Jeronimas Kacinskas, joined the faculty in 1967 on the recommendation of John Bavicchi. The Lithuanian-born composer conducted the Vilnius Philharmonic and the Vilnius State Opera until 1944, when he fled on foot from Stalin's invading armies. After a hazardous odyssey that took him through war-torn Czechoslovakia, Kacinskas ended up in an American-run displaced persons camp in Germany. In 1949, with the help of Americans he met in the camp, he moved to the United States and began the process of learning a new language and building a new career. Settling in Boston, he took a job playing organ and directing the choir at St. Peter's Lithuanian Church in South Boston, before Bavicchi helped him get a position teaching conducting and composition at Berklee. "When Berklee needed a conducting teacher, I felt someone of his caliber would really benefit the college," Bavicchi says. Kacinskas retired from Berklee in 1986.

Mick Goodrick as a student.

Gabor Szabo conducts a clinic.

Gabor Szabo with Mick Goodrick, then a faculty member, and President Lawrence Berk during a 1968 visit.

Guitarist Gabor Szabo returned to his alma mater in 1968 and discovered that Berklee was profoundly different from the school he knew in the late 1950s, when there were few guitarists and no guitar major. Szabo had fled his native Hungary after the Soviet Union crushed the revolution in 1956, and had come to Berklee. After leaving Berklee in 1960, Szabo had played with vibraphonist Gary McFarland, drummer Chico Hamilton, and saxophonist Charles Lloyd. His music began to incorporate rock and blues after 1969. He died in 1982.

Guitarist Mick Goodrick, whose class Szabo visited, taught at Berklee for four years after graduating in 1967. He played with Gary Burton's groups between 1973 and 1975, including an influential quintet that also featured Pat Metheny. A much sought-after private guitar instructor, Goodrick has also recorded with Charlie Haden and Jack DeJohnnette. His recordings as a leader have featured saxophonist Gerry Bergonzi and Berklee faculty members, drummer Gary Chaffee and bassist Bruce Gertz, among others.

The Dues Band in WGBH studios for their Christmas 1968, broadcast. The band included future faculty members Bill Pierce '73 (seated at far right), and trombonists Hal Crook '71 (second from left) and Tony Lada '72 (third from left). Alto saxophonist Richie Cole is seated in the saxophone section second from left.

Charlie Mariano plays nathasvaram during a Radio Malaya broadcast in 1967 (above, left) and with the Concert Jazz Orchestra at the 1968 *Boston Globe* Jazz Festival (above). Rick Laird is the bassist in the Berklee ensemble.

In December 1968, Phil Wilson and the Dues Band played jazz settings of Christmas songs for a studio audience of children at WGBH. Wilson founded the Dues Band in 1965. "The first Dues Band was actually called the Animal Band," Wilson remembers. "That's what the guys in the band were called; they were a pretty rowdy bunch. Thank God, you do grow up! I just got together all of the guys who wanted to play their own music after school. After that first year, I changed the name. I wanted to make the point that there is no time in your life when you don't pay some kind of dues. And if anyone thinks that as soon as you graduate from Berklee, life is going to be rosy, they have another thing coming."

Earlier in the year, another of Berklee's premier ensembles also made a public appearance. Herb Pomeroy's Concert Jazz Orchestra with guest soloist Charlie Mariano, opened for the Wes Montgomery Quintet and the Duke Ellington Orchestra at the *Boston Globe* Jazz Festival in February 1968. (Pomeroy's ensemble was also called the Recording Band, but when they played in concert, they were called the Concert Jazz Orchestra.) Mariano was featured on the nathasvaram, an Indian reed instrument he studied while on leave from Berklee to coach and rehearse the Malayan radio and television orchestra, just as Herb Pomeroy had done several years earlier. The Concert Jazz Orchestra's bassist was Rick Laird '69, who later played in the Mahavishnu Orchestra with fellow student Jan Hammer '69.

	1968 Chick Corea joins the Miles Davis Group.	Ellington performs Second Sacred Concert in New York.	Anthony Braxton records double album of solo saxophone *For Alto*.	
1968 The Fifth Dimension's "Up, Up, and Away" earns six Grammys.	Jimmy Page forms Led Zeppelin.	Steppenwolf releases "Born to Be Wild."	Sly and the Family Stone release "Dance to the Music."	The Beatles release their biggest-selling single "Hey, Jude."
			1968 Wendy Carlos uses the Moog synthesizer to create "Switched-On Bach."	

Gary Burton rehearsing Carla Bley's *A Genuine Tong Funeral* for an appearance on WGBH. The group included Berklee students Alan Broadbent, piano; Tony Lada, trombone; Alex Elin, tenor saxophone; Ronald Smith '69, tuba; Harry Drabkin '69, saxophone; Rolf Johnson '69, trumpet. Burton's quartet included Steve Swallow, bass; Jerry Hahn, guitar; Bill Goodwin, drums.

In February 1969, Gary Burton returned to Berklee to conduct a workshop, assembling a group of students to augment his quartet for a televised performance of jazz composer Carla Bley's extended work *A Genuine Tong Funeral*, which he recorded in 1967. In 1964, Burton had been Berklee's first visiting artist. Clinics and workshops conducted by guest artists would eventually become an important part of the Berklee educational experience.

The Berklee students Burton assembled for the WGBH broadcast included pianist Alan Broadbent '69, who was the first recipient of the Richard Levy Memorial Award, given annually to an outstanding student composer. New Zealand native Broadbent graduated from Berklee and immediately went with the Woody Herman orchestra. He later led his own trios and was a member of Charlie Haden's Quartet West. Other students in the ensemble later became Berklee faculty members. Alex Elin '69 began teaching at Berklee in 1976; and Tony Lada in 1972.

Berklee faculty applaud a band at the first New England High School Stage Band Festival.

In spring of 1969, Lee Eliot Berk founded the first annual New England High School Stage Band Festival. A Berklee planning team worked with the Massachusetts Association of Jazz Educators, a Massachusetts state chapter of the National Association of Jazz Educators (NAJE), organized by Berk and John LaPorta.

The first festival attracted 15 bands from New England and New York. In 1995, the festival attracted 170 bands and also encompassed small jazz and vocal ensembles. During the festival's years of greatest growth, from 1971 to 1992, current Director of Administrative Auxilary Services Norman Silver served as festival director. Over the years literally thousands of talented high school students have participated in the festival, benefiting from the performance evaluations, clinics and workshops, teaching demonstrations, and prize and scholarship award opportunities.

Massachusetts educators met with Berklee representatives to organize the first New England High School Stage Band Festival. Berklee representatives on the left side of the table are (standing, from left to right): Gerald Siddons, Andy McGhee, Joe Viola, and Jack Weaver, and (seated, from left to right) Ted Pease, Lee Eliot Berk, Phil Wilson, and John LaPorta.

The first executive committee of the Faculty Association (from left to right): Alan Dawson, Lee Eliot Berk, Gerald Siddons, Joe Viola, Michael Rendish, Dave Matayabas, and Ray Kotwica.

Alma, Lawrence, and Lee Eliot Berk at the 1967 Commencement.

Lee Eliot Berk began working at Berklee after earning a law degree from Boston University. He served in a number of positions, including bursar and supervisor of the Private Study Division, and as his contributions continued to broaden, he was appointed vice president. Applying his legal training to the Berklee curriculum, he developed an elective course in music law that became the basis for his ASCAP-Deems Taylor Award-winning book *Legal Protection for the Creative Musician*. He also helped organize the Faculty Association and served on its executive committee. The Faculty Association sponsored the Berklee concert series, administered the community outreach program, and provided crisis health support for the faculty.

	1969 Miles Davis records *Bitches Brew*.	Herbie Hancock records *The Prisoner*.	The Art Ensemble of Chicago record *People in Sorrow*.	
1969 400,000 attend Woodstock, "three days of peace, love, and music."	The Who release the first rock opera *Tommy*.	The Jackson 5 have their first #1 hit "I Want You Back."	Chicago and Blood, Sweat, and Tears popularize jazz-rock.	The Beatles perform together for the last time during filming of *Let It Be*.
		1969 Lejaren Hiller and John Cage use Illiac, a large mainframe computer, to make compositional decisions to produce the multimedia extravaganze "HPSCHD."		Alan R. Pearlman develops his ARP modular voltage-controlled synthesizer.

Lee Eliot Berk (right), with Lawrence Berk, student Johari Salleh, and Charlie Mariano.

As a young faculty member, Ted Pease leads an in-class analysis of a score.

1970 Singer/songwriter James Taylor releases "Fire and Rain."

Joni Mitchell releases "Big Yellow Taxi."

The Grateful Dead release debut single "Uncle John's Band."

The Allman Brothers, ZZ Top, and the Cha Daniels Band popularize southern rock.

Ted Pease.

A 1969 student ensemble directed by Ted Pease featured Gary Anderson and Harry Drabkin, reeds; Jaxon Stock '71, trombone; Mick Goodrick, electric bass; Ted Siebs '71, drums; and Vicki von Eps, piano.

As the student population increased between 1966 and 1969, the need for new course offerings grew more apparent. "After school closed down and they gave the ensemble rooms over to the students to practice and rehearse in, that's when a lot of the new music was heard," Associate Dean of Faculty Ronald Bentley remembers. "A lot of the younger students coming directly out of high school were rock players. During the day they'd learn jazz in the classroom. Then at night, they would play what they wanted to, but they'd put a little of the jazz thing onto it. At times it seemed like two schools going on simultaneously."

The leadership of redesigning the writing and arranging curriculum to reflect the increasing prominence of rock music fell primarily to Ted Pease. "We had to branch out into new areas and satisfy the needs of new students who were interested in more than jazz," Pease says. "We had to offer more electives—in rock, and pop, jingle writing, and arranging in the rock idiom."

Pease came to Berklee as a student in 1962, after earning a B.A. in English from Cornell University. "Bob Share offered me a teaching position while I finished my last year," Pease remembers. "I split my senior year into two years, and graduated with the class of 1966." As chair of the Arranging Department and later as first chair of the Professional Writing Division, Pease continued to steer the Berklee curriculum in innovative directions. During his tenure as division chair, Berklee instituted the first college-level songwriting major and expanded writing and arranging course offerings to include a wide array of contemporary music styles. Pease stepped down from his administrative duties in 1991 to return to his first love, teaching. In recognition of his years of service to the Berklee community, he was appointed the college's first distinguished professor.

1970 Maynard Ferguson releases a jazz-rock version of "MacArthur Park."	Miles Davis records *Jack Johnson* and *Live/Evil*.	Max Roach forms percussion ensemble M'Boom.	Herbie Hancock records *Mwandishi*.
Jimi Hendrix and Janis Joplin die.	The Beatles disband.	Aerosmith forms.	
1970 Commercial production begins of 16-track, 2-inch tape recorders.	The first quadraphonic discs are released.	Portable voltage-controlled instruments such as the Minimoog and ARP 2600 are introduced.	

Michael Rendish and Don Wilkins discuss their score for the PBS special "America by Design."

Michael Rendish explains the workings of a synthesizer to a class of visiting high school students.

As the founding chair of the Harmony Department, Michael Rendish also played a large part in the transformation of the Berklee curriculum. "Looking at the harmony curriculum, I thought it didn't reflect trends that had exploded in popular music since the coming of the Beatles," Rendish says. "I felt we needed to address what was going on harmonically in popular music. So I put together some things and Bob Share okayed it.

"We had a very different structure in the administration," Rendish continues. "We survived because we were very, very loose. It was not at all unusual for me to call Gerry Siddons, who was then dean of scheduling, tell him my course idea. He'd write a description, give it a number in the catalog, and we taught it. It was not only acceptable, but it worked."

Rendish came to Berklee on a *Down Beat* scholarship in 1961 and shared a dorm room with upperclassman Gary Burton his first year. A member of the class of 1966, Rendish began teaching in his senior year. He also initiated the electronic music program at Berklee in 1971. While heading the electronic music program he grew increasingly involved in film scoring. In 1984, when the Music Synthesis Department was created, he became assistant chair of the Film Scoring Department.

Michael Rendish teaching a harmony class during a summer session for music educators.

A rehearsal of Charlie Mariano's international student ensemble was filmed for a USIA documentary about Berklee in 1969. Members included Justo Almaria on tenor saxophone and Chris Hinze on flute.

As Berklee approached its 25th anniversary, many kinds of music were heard in the school's recital halls and practice rooms. Charlie Mariano's ensemble of international students, which included Dutch flutist Chris Hinze and Mexican saxophonist Justo Almario, played jazz arrangement of folk music of other countries. Hinze later led his own group, the Chris Hinze Combination, which used both jazz and baroque classical influences. Almario recorded under his own name and played with percussionist Mongo Santamaria, Cuban bassist Israel "Cachao" Lopez, and other Latin jazz figures.

Blues and rock were played at Berklee and in Boston-area clubs by bands such as Swallow, which featured Berklee students. At the 1969 annual Christmas concert, Phil Wilson and the Dues Band became the first student ensemble at Berklee to play the music of James Brown. The concert also featured music of the Beatles and contemporary classical composer Jacob Druckman. A student jazz-rock ensemble under Wilson's direction featured bassist Abraham Laboriel, Sr., and drummer Harvey Mason. Mason later became one of the most sought-after studio musicians in Los Angeles and was featured on jazz-pop crossover hits such as Herbie Hancock's "Chameleon" and George Benson's "Breezin'."

Herb Pomeroy's Recording Band continued to feature Berklee's best jazz students. In 1969 the band included Harvie Schwartz on bass and Larry Monroe on alto saxophone. Swartz went on to perform and record as a leader and as a sideman with pianist Steve Kuhn, vocalist Sheila Jordan, and many others. Larry Monroe started teaching at Berklee in 1970 and became chair of the Professional Performance Division in 1985.

The student jazz-rock ensemble under Phil Wilson's direction with bassist Abraham Laboriel, Sr., and drummer Harvey Mason.

Phil Wilson and singer Eric Butler perform James Brown's "Mother Popcorn" at the annual Christmas concert in 1969.

In 1969, the Recording Band featured Harvie Swartz on bass and Larry Monroe on alto saxophone.

A Condor Sound Modulator is seen at the far right on stage next to faculty
trumpeter Lennie Johnson. Other featured faculty soloists in the concert were
John Laporta (far left) and Andy McGhee (standing in front of the band
between LaPorta and Wilson).

In February 1970, Phil Wilson conducted a concert to show off the capabilities of the
Condor Sound Modulator, which electronically modified the sound of one instrument to
resemble another. A big band with faculty soloists Lennie Johnson, Andy McGhee, and
John LaPorta performed compositions by Kendall Capps, William Leavitt, and Wilson,
all of which made use of the Condor Sound Modulator.

Jazz pianist and educator Billy Taylor (far right) hands a diploma to a graduating student at the 1970 Commencement.

The President and Board of Trustees
of the
Berklee School of Music
are pleased to announce
that through the authority of the
Board of Higher Education
of the
Commonwealth of Massachusetts
This Institution shall
hereafter be known as
Berklee College of Music

Boston
Massachusetts

In May 1970, jazz pianist and educator Billy Taylor addressed the largest graduating class Berklee had yet produced. With mushrooming enrollment, an innovative curriculum, and creative faculty, the future of the 25-year-old college looked very bright indeed. In June, the name of the school was changed to Berklee College of Music to better reflect its educational scope and stature.

Chapter Four

Berklee College of Music
1970 – 1979

At the beginning of the 1970s, both rock and jazz were in transition. The Beatles broke up. Jimi Hendrix and Janis Joplin died. Singer/songwriters such as James Taylor, Joni Mitchell, and Van Morrison brought a new intimacy and sophistication to popular songs. The southern blues-rock of the Allman Brothers and ZZ Top grew popular. Miles Davis outraged jazz traditionalists with amplified jazz-rock.

Berklee mirrored the surrounding musical tumult and diversity. In many ways, the 1970s marked a significant expansion of Berklee's evolution from "the jazz school" to a school that accommodated a broader spectrum of contemporary music. Its popular image as "the guitar school" significantly belied the wide range of activity in jazz, film music, recording technology, and songwriting at the college. Barriers were falling, and Berklee students were doing their share of breaking them down.

Students Mike Stern '75, Jay Azolina '76, and Mitch Coodley '75 in faculty member Pat Metheny's guitar ensemble at the 1975 Commencement concert.

1971 Louis Armstrong dies.

Anthony Braxton, Chick Corea, Dave Holland, and Barry Altschul form Circle.

Weather Report releases self-titled debut album.

Mahavishnu Orchestra records *The Inner Mounting Flame.*

1971 Carole King's debut album *Tapestry* tops the charts for 15 weeks.

Emerson, Lake, and Palmer release their self-titled debut.

Issac Hayes releases #1 hit "Theme From Shaft."

Marvin Gaye releases *What's Goin' On.*

1971 Commercial production begins of 24-track, 2-inch tape recorders.

Faculty member Charlie Mariano (seated, wearing hat) rehearses a student ensemble with (from left to right) Gary Anderson, Mick Goodrick, Jaxon Stock '72, Vicki von Eps '71, Abraham Laboriel, Sr., Jon Klein '72, and Harry Blazer '72.

Faculty member Frank Turziano's guitar ensemble exemplified the eclectic atmosphere at Berklee. Its performances drew on classical, jazz, funk, blues, and rock influences. "The guitar ensemble up to that point had really been just a way to learn to play; it wasn't performance-oriented at all," says faculty member Charles Chapman, a member of the ensemble. "But in this group, everybody just clicked, so Frank kept it together from 1969 to 1972, and we played concerts at high schools and elsewhere." Turziano was later coordinator of ensemble programs from 1977 to 1981 and director of the Berklee Performance Center from 1981 to 1993.

Faculty member Charlie Mariano also encouraged student interest in new music. Laugh and Cry, his student band during the 1970-71 academic year, mixed rock and jazz influences with some world music, but an official Berklee Jazz-Rock Ensemble was still two years away.

Frank Turziano '69 directs the Berklee Guitar Ensemble, with (from left to right) Fred Oshiro '72, Mike Ihde '72, Abraham Laboriel, Sr., Jerry Montone '72, Charles Chapman '72, Jon Damian '74, and Mike Grady '71 at the 1971 Commencement concert.

Dr. Albert Sloane.

Rod Nordell.

Mabel Hamilton.

The Board of Trustees welcomed three new members in the first half of 1971. In February, journalist Roderick Nordell and attorney Herbert Baer were elected to the board. Nordell, Arts Editor of the *Christian Science Monitor*, was still a member of the board in 1995 and served as trustee representative on the 50th Anniversary Executive Leadership Committee. In May, ophthalmologist Dr. Albert Sloane was elected to the board. At the time of his election, Dr. Sloane was the senior consulting surgeon of the Massachusetts Eye and Ear Infirmary and assistant clinical professor of ophthalmology at the Harvard Medical School.

The board continued to grow throughout the decade. In 1976, banker Mabel Hamilton became the first woman to join the board. In 1977, William Davis, a senior vice president at the investment firm Donaldson, Lufkin, and Jenrette, and Allan McLean, from United Investment Counsel, were elected.

113

Commencement speaker Atlantic Records Vice President Arif Mardin and Duke Ellington.

Duke Ellington steps away from the podium after concluding his remarks upon receiving the first honorary doctorate awarded by Berklee.

The world's hippest reception pianist.

On May 21, 1971, Berklee bestowed its first honorary degree on Duke Ellington. On Commencement day, President Lawrence Berk introduced Duke saying, "There is no aspect of modern American music and jazz that has not felt the impact of his unique talent." At the reception afterwards, Duke supplied the entertainment, playing piano and taking requests from guests.

Arif Mardin, then recently promoted to vice president at Atlantic Records, delivered the Commencement address at this milestone ceremony. "You must never stop learning and perfecting your art even after the time you start to reap the rewards of your hard-earned career," he said. "You must ask the same questions of yourselves: did I do my best, did I explore all the possibilities, did I give this project my undivided attention?"

114

| 1972 | Weather Report records *I Sing the Body Electric.* | Chick Corea forms Return to Forever. | Gato Barbieri wins Grammy for *Last Tango in Paris* soundtrack. | Art Ensemble of Chicago record *Bap-Tizm* at Ann Arbor Jazz and Blues Festival. |

| 1972 | Philadelphia Soul/Gamble & Huff Records become popular. | Neil Young releases country-rock album *Harvest.* | Don McLean's hit single "American Pie" is #1 on the charts for 7 weeks. | Steely Dan debuts with jazz-rock influenced *Can't Buy a Thrill.* |

Duke Ellington sits with Alma and Lawrence Berk during a break at Paul's Mall.

President Berk reminisces with baritone saxophonist Harry Carney, a childhood friend.

Earlier in the week prior to Commencement, the Ellington Orchestra played at Paul's Mall, a club just blocks down Boylston Street from the college. Lawrence and Alma Berk were Ellington's guests one night and Duke dedicated "Satin Doll" to Mrs. Berk. Backstage, President Berk chatted with his childhood neighbor and English High classmate, baritone saxophonist Harry Carney.

The 16-piece Buddy Rich band that played the 1971 Newport Jazz Festival featured 10 Berklee alumni, including a saxophone section with (left to right) Pat LaBarbara, Richie Cole, and Jimmy Mosher, and (on the extreme right, playing baritone) Joe Calo.

In early July, Alma and Lawrence Berk attended the 1971 Newport Jazz Festival, where an especially large number of Berklee alumni performed. The 16-piece Buddy Rich band included 10 former Berklee students: Pat LaBarbara '67, Richie Cole, Joe Calo '68, and Jimmy Mosher in the saxophone section; Jeff Stout '68, Lin Biviano '67, and Joe Georgiani '67 on trumpet; Tony Lada '72 and Tony DiMaggio on trombone; and bassist Paul Kondziela '70. In addition, faculty member Alan Dawson performed with the Dave Brubeck Quartet, and former faculty member, tenor saxophonist Junior Cook appeared with Freddie Hubbard's quintet. Bill Chase '58 also led his jazz-rock fusion band Chase. Other Berklee alumni on stage that weekend included trumpeter Jack Walrath '67 with Ray Charles, guitarist Sonny Sharrock '62 with Herbie Mann, and drummer Harvey Mason '68 with George Shearing.

Faculty member Alan Dawson on drums with baritone saxophonist Gerry Mulligan, bassist Jack Six, and pianist Dave Brubeck at the 1971 Newport Jazz Festival.

Trumpeter Bill Chase with his jazz-rock fusion band
Chase at the 1971 Newport Jazz Festival.

During his first semester teaching at Berklee, Gary Burton appeared as a special guest at the annual Christmas concert by Phil Wilson and the Dues Band.

The Gary Burton Quartet, featuring Berklee alumni Mick Goodrick on guitar and Ted Siebs on drums, plus Steve Swallow, who joined the Berklee faculty in September 1974, on electric bass.

Gary Burton conducting a private lesson.

Gary Burton with pianist Makoto Ozone and Steve Swallow.

Faculty hiring increased to keep pace with growing enrollment. Among those joining in the fall of 1971 was Gary Burton, who had an immediate impact on the college. A pioneer of jazz-rock fusion, Burton encouraged students to explore in that direction. He introduced fresh material to ensemble classes and kept dozens of lead sheets, which he urged students to study and play, in his famous tune file. "I copied out tunes I thought were hip by Chick Corea, Keith Jarrett, Carla Bley, and Steve Swallow and told students to just come by and take what they liked," says Burton, who was promoted to dean of curriculum in 1985.

After joining the faculty, Burton remained an active performer whose music grew increasingly popular with both audiences and critics. His solo album *Alone at Last* won a Grammy in 1971 and *Duet*, recorded with Chick Corea, earned one in 1978. A second duet with Corea, *Concert in Munich*, earned a Grammy in 1981. Many of his most highly regarded groups featured Berklee faculty and students. Saxophonists Jim Odgren '75 and Don McCaslin '88, drummer Ted Siebs '72, trumpeter Tiger Okoshi '75, pianist Makoto Ozone '83, and guitarist Wolfgang Muthspiel '90 were some of the students Burton recruited into his groups over the years. In addition, faculty members Mick Goodrick, Pat Metheny, and Steve Swallow were members of his bands.

119

As a student, Stephany Tiernan (left) gave lessons to Boston-area school children on Saturdays through the Community Service Program.

Community Service Program participants traveled to Norfolk prison to give lessons to inmates in 1973.

Tom van der Geld '73 plays for some Boston school students during a Community Service Program concert.

In September 1971, Berklee formalized and strengthened its ties to the Boston community with the creation of the Community Service Program. The program sent student ensembles to entertain in hospitals, correctional institutions, and public schools. On Saturdays, the college invited area public school students in for private lessons with Berklee upperclass students. "Tutoring on Saturdays was wonderful," says Stephany Tiernan '74, who worked for the program as a student. "It gave me my first real teaching experience." Tiernan, who joined the faculty in 1975, became the first woman to hold a department leadership position at Berklee when she was appointed assistant chair of the Piano Department in 1990.

During the "Interplay" concert, faculty drummer Joe Hunt listens through headphones to a click track that synchronized him with a tape of synthesized music by Michael Rendish.

Michael Rendish (left) plays electric piano during the first concert at Berklee to feature the ARP synthesizer. The synthesizer sits on a table in the background. Human performers include Jon Klein '71 on baritone saxophone, Alan Michalek '72 on tenor saxophone, and Jaxon Stock on trombone.

While new styles of contemporary music made their way into Berklee ensembles and classrooms, faculty member Michael Rendish introduced a new instrument to the college, the synthesizer. Synthesizers made their public debut at Berklee on November 11, 1971, in a concert entitled "Interplay," organized by Rendish. "Interplay" featured an acoustic quintet accompanied by a tape of music created on the synthesizer by Rendish.

Berklee purchased its first synthesizer, an ARP 2500, in the summer of 1970, and Rendish taught the first electronic music course that fall. "It was Dick Bobbitt who should get credit for turning the ignition key on getting synthesizers to Berklee," says Rendish. "He found out about a course at Catholic University in Washington and he drove down and back to interview H. Emerson Myers, the composer and teacher who conducted the class. When he came back, he said, 'Take a look at this. I'm sure there is a way Berklee can use it.' So I took a seminar with Myers, and on the plane back I wrote the course for the first semester and worked out a list of equipment. It was the first program to emphasize mainstream uses for the instrument, rather than the esoteric art music that was being written for it at the time."

Current Professor of Percussion Joe Hunt, in his first semester on the Berklee faculty, played drums for "Interplay." Hunt, who had recorded and performed with composer George Russell, pianist Bill Evans, and many others, was recommended for the faculty by Gary Burton, who had met and played with him in the quartet of Stan Getz.

123

Alan Broadbent (left) and big band leader Woody Herman talk with students during an October 1971 visit.

In late October 1971, Woody Herman paid one of his frequent visits to Berklee. Nearly 25 years after his big band placed first in the Schillinger House student poll, Herman was keeping pace with changing musical tastes, in part through his connection to Berklee and its students. Pianist Alan Broadbent '69 was one of five Berklee alumni in Herman's band when Herman arrived for a question-and-answer session with students. Herman also dropped in on former band members Phil Wilson and Andy McGhee.

Phil Wilson and Woody Herman meet during Herman's 1971 visit.

| **1973** | Ellington's Third Sacred Concert is performed at Westminster Abby. | Chuck Mangione releases *Land of Make Believe.* |

| **1973** | Pink Floyd releases *Dark Side of the Moon.* | Southern rock band Lynyrd Skynyrd releases their debut hit "Freebird." | Worldwide broadcast of Elvis Presley concert is seen by largest audience in rock history. | Aerosmith release debut album. | Alice Cooper releases *Billion Dollar Babies.* |

| **1973** | AM/FM radios become standard in American-built automobiles. |

Lawrence, Lee Eliot, and Alma Berk at the 1971 ASCAP-Deems Taylor Award ceremony.

At the end of the fall semester, in December 1971, Lee Eliot Berk, who was then vice president of the college, received first prize in the fourth annual ASCAP-Deems Taylor Awards for his book *Legal Protection for the Creative Musician*. The book had its origins in a class, Legal Protection of Musical Materials, taught by Berk, who organized his lecture notes into the awarding-winning text. In the book, subjects such as copyright, performance rights, and licensing agreements were approached from a musician's perspective. Other business-oriented courses, such as Record Marketing and Promotion, the General Business of Music (which Gary Burton taught for several years), and Entrepreneurship, were gradually introduced, until a new Music Business/Management major was offered at Berklee in 1992.

Ornette Coleman and Prime Time record *Dancing in Your Head.*

Miles Davis records *On the Corner.*

Toshiko Akiyoshi and Lew Tabackin Big Band record debut album *Kogun.*

Jimmy Smith plays during a March 1972 workshop.

Visiting artist clinics, which started with Gary Burton, grew into a Berklee tradition and really began flourishing in the 1970s. In March 1972, jazz pianist Oscar Peterson spent a day touring the school, meeting faculty, inspecting Michael Rendish's synthesizer, and talking with students.

Earlier that same month, students crowded into a workshop by one of the most popular hard bop musicians of the day, Hammond B-3 wizard Jimmy Smith, who pioneered the use of organ in modern jazz.

Oscar Peterson talks with students during his 1972 visit to Berklee.

Arthur Fiedler receives his honorary
degree from Lawrence Berk.

The trumpet section of Herb Pomeroy's Concert Jazz
Orchestra at the 1972 Commencement concert.

Boston Pops conductor Arthur Fiedler received an honorary doctorate at the 1972
Commencement ceremony. Fiedler held the music directorship of an American orchestra longer than any other person, leading the Boston Pops Orchestra from 1930 until his
death in 1979. Under his direction, the Boston Pops earned both artistic and commercial
success and became a model for similar orchestras throughout the United States. "This
man, probably unknowingly, is responsible in large measure for the growth and freedom
of musical expression which is so vital to the educational philosophy here at Berklee,"
said Lawrence Berk in his introductory remarks.

Herb Pomeroy's Concert Jazz Orchestra performed at the Commencement concert
immediately following. Some members later became Berklee faculty. Among them were:
Richard Appleman '72, later chair of the Bass Department, and trombonist Tony Lada.
Other students in the band included drummer Ted Siebs and trumpeter Herb Robertson
'72, who went on to play and record as a leader and with Tim Berne and other leading
jazz avant-gardists of the 1980s and 1990s.

Phil Wilson conducts the Dues Band and members of the Boston Symphony Orchestra in the world premiere of his tone poem *The Earth's Children*.

The winter 1972 concert schedule included the first of many collaborations between Berklee and the Boston Symphony Orchestra's Youth Concert Series at Symphony Hall. Founded in 1959 by Harry Ellis Dickson, the Youth Concert Series presented classical music programs designed to educate and entertain children. At the concert in November 1972, Phil Wilson conducted the world premiere of *The Earth's Children*, with featured soloists Jan Konopasek '78 on tenor saxophone and Tony Klatka '74 on trombone. His six-part tone poem for symphony orchestra and jazz ensemble depicted the "moods and conflicts of today's youth in his struggle for maturity." The inspiration for the piece came from "seeing students from all over the world coming to Berklee," Wilson says. A 1981 revival of the work featured saxophonist Greg Osby '83 and trombonist Frank Lacy '81 in the soloist roles, with Herve Legrand '81, son of composer and pianist Michel Legrand, on keyboard.

Other Berklee-Boston Symphony Orchestra collaborations in the Youth Concert Series included a performance of Mike Gibbs' *Liturgy* conducted by Herb Pomeroy in 1975. In January 1976, William Maloof, chair of the Composition Department, premiered his composition *Concerto in Tribus Linguis* (*Concerto in Three Languages*), which combined the symphony orchestra with a rock group and jazz ensemble.

Composition Department Chair
William Maloof conducts the premiere
of *Concerto in Tribus Linguis.*

As a student, Richard Appleman played electric bass guitar in a big band led by trombonist Tony Lada (standing) in January 1972.

Many Berklee curriculum innovations were developed by alumni who were hired as faculty members. This was the case with the electric bass major offered by the Bass Department. Richard Appleman joined the faculty in June 1972 and the next year began creating an electric bass major with the help of faculty bassists Steve Swallow and John Repucci. "Before that time, instruction in the department was mostly traditional double bass and mainstream jazz," Appleman says. "In the mid-1970s, we really tapped into the contemporary jazz bass and the electric rock-fusion styles." Appleman, who was also a founding member of the Fringe, a free jazz trio with current Assistant Professor of Woodwinds George Garzone '72 and drummer Bob Guillotti '72, was appointed chair of the Bass Department in 1981.

In 1977, Tony Teixeira (left) led Four Bass Hit, a faculty band featuring Bass Department members Richard Appleman, Bruce Gertz, and John Repucci, and current Piano Department Chair Paul Schmeling.

John Scofield on guitar
with the Dues Band at the
1972 Christmas concert.

Among the students in the 1972 Christmas concert by Phil Wilson's Dues Band was guitarist John Scofield '73, who later became one of the preeminent guitarists in jazz. Miles Davis tapped Scofield as his guitarist in 1982 and he also played in Marc Johnson's Bass Desires with Bill Frisell '77. In the 1990s, he led a quartet featuring Joe Lovano '72 on tenor saxophone, and made albums with Frisell and Pat Metheny.

"The most important thing about Berklee for me was the people—the other musicians and the teachers," Scofield said in a 1992 interview for *Berklee today*. "Also, the curriculum was great for me, because I didn't know how to read that well. . . . I often think about where I would be if I hadn't gone to school. I know I would have gotten to the same place. But, I think I got here quick because of that big dose of music theory."

133

Alto saxophonist Cannonball Adderley at a clinic in March 1973.

Khalid Yasin (Larry Young) and his trio perform in a clinic in July 1973.

Guest clinicians and artists-in-residence spanned an ever-widening musical spectrum. In September 1972, guitarist Larry Coryell conducted a workshop with three members of his band: saxophonist Steve Marcus, bassist John Miller, and electric pianist Mike Mandel. Coryell was a member of Gary Burton's first quartet, led the widely influential fusion band Eleventh House in the early 1970s, and a jazz quartet with pianist Stanley Cowell in the 1980s.

Saxophonist Cannonball Adderley conducted a workshop in March 1973. Adderley recorded with Miles Davis on *Kind of Blue* and later led one of the 1960s' most influential and popular soul jazz quintets.

Rhythm and blues-influenced jazz was represented by two of its best-selling artists. In March, flutist Bobbi Humphrey became the first woman to conduct a documented clinic at the college. The immensely popular saxophonist Grover Washington, Jr., was a guest lecturer and performer in September 1973.

Organist Khalid Yasin (Larry Young), who created a place for the Hammond B-3 in modal and free jazz with his own groups, and in jazz-rock fusion with Tony Williams' Lifetime, visited in July 1973 for a clinic.

Bobbi Humphrey, Berklee's first woman visiting artist.

1974 Duke Ellington dies.	The National Jazz Ensemble performs at Allice Tully Hall.	The New York Jazz Repertory Company performs at Carnegie Hall.	Pat Metheny joins Gary Burton's band.	Weather Report finish recording *Mysterious Traveler.*
	1974 "Middle-of-the-road" artists such as Helen Reddy, Abba, and John Denver dominate the top 40.		Paul McCartney and Wings release *Band on the Run.*	
			1974 Tom Oberheim introduces instruments with limited polyphony and some ability to store sound parameters in computer memory.	

Larry Coryell and alumnus Steve
Marcus at a Berklee clinic in 1972.

During the 1978 Boston Sackbut Week, Tom Plsek, Phil Wilson, and Tom Everett made Lawrence Berk an "honorary trombone player for life" and presented him with a plaque and an original portrait in appreciation for his efforts on behalf of the International Trombone Association event.

Berklee trombonists Phil Wilson, Rick Stepton '68, Lennie Peterson '79, and Mike Gibbs appear with Jeff Friedman '79 and his orchestra at a 1981 Sackbut Week concert.

In April 1973, Phil Wilson and Tom Everett, a faculty member from Harvard University, organized the first annual Sackbut Week, a celebration of trombone music named after a predecessor of the modern trombone. "The idea was to create an ecumenical week for trombone players that would include all kinds of music for trombones, from across the spectrum," Wilson says.

Ensembles and individuals from Boston-area and New England public schools, colleges, and universities, as well as guest lecturers from New York City's Metropolitan Opera, the Boston Symphony Orchestra, and the BBC Orchestra joined in the seven-day celebration. Between 1973 and 1986, Sackbut Week presented over 200 events, including world premieres of new works for trombone, concerts on historic instruments, jam sessions, radio broadcasts, and lectures. Special guests included jazz greats like Vic Dickenson in 1974, Slide Hampton in 1977, Jimmy Knepper in 1978, and new music composer-performers Stuart Dempster in 1976 and George Lewis in 1981.

Students and faculty from many schools participated in Sackbut Week, but over time the festival increasingly focused on the Berklee trombone community. Many Sackbut Week events, including the final Clean-Up Day, with its schedule of lectures, workshops, and performances, took place at Berklee. Phil Wilson, Tom Plsek, Tony Lada, John Licata '70, and Mike Gibbs all led ensembles, contributed new works, and helped organize the event. "There has never been anything like it for trombonists, before or since," says Plsek.

Phil Wilson leads 76 trombones out onto the field at Fenway Park for a pregame performance in 1977.

In 1978, Phil Wilson conducted Sackbut Week participants in a free outdoor concert beside the locomotive at the Boston Museum of Science. Jazz trombonist Steve Turre (center, wearing knit cap) is special guest.

3713

Harry Ellis Dickson (right) received an
honorary degree in 1973.

Violinist and conductor Harry Ellis Dickson, a member of the Boston Symphony Orchestra
since 1938, received an honorary degree at the 1973 Commencement. Founder and music
director of the Youth Concert Series and assistant conductor of the Boston Pops and
Esplanade orchestras, Dickson told the graduating class, "There is no room in music for
snobbery. Music—all music—should be judged on its own merit and value."

VETERANS MEMORIAL AUDITORIUM
FRIDAY AND SATURDAY, NOVEMBER 23, 24
AT 8:00 P. M.

TONY BENNETT

IN CONCERT WITH

BERKLEE COLLEGE CONCERT JAZZ ORCHESTRA

MUSICAL DIRECTOR - TORRIE ZITO

TICKETS: $10.00, $8.00, $6.00

ON SALE: LADD'S MUSIC CENTERS - - - 942-1160
ROTH TICKET AGENCY - - - 751-0200
TICKET ENDOWMENT - - - 884-3051
THE ECHO, 243 Atwells Ave. - 521-5760

Faculty trumpeter Herb Pomeroy and student Tiger Okoshi duet as singer Tony Bennett listens.

In November and December 1973, the Berklee Concert Jazz Orchestra participated in a unique concert tour. The band accompanied singer Tony Bennett on a swing through several East Coast cities. At each concert, the band played an opening set, then backed Bennett, who gave students solo spots on several tunes. Bennett, a remarkably consistent singer of popular songs, made occasional forays into jazz, most notably with the Count Basie Orchestra and in two duet recordings with pianist Bill Evans. He enjoyed a surprising popularity among younger listeners in the mid-1990s. His daughter Antonia, also a singer, attended Berklee, starting in 1992.

139

Aimee Mann '80.

Patty Larkin '74 and Bruce Cockburn '65.

GOOD LIFE TO YOU
music & lyrics by Laura Stills

Love's so unfair

Never really ours to share

But we played the game,

Never thought we'd lose.

   Good life to you.

Throughout the 1970s, Berklee faculty increasingly looked to new developments in contemporary American popular music for the subjects of new courses. A growing awareness of the importance of songwriters in rock and pop music led to the creation of the
first college-level songwriting course, offered for the first time during the 1973-74 academic year. The idea for the course came from Jon Aldrich '74, who was then a student
and later became an associate professor of Songwriting. Faculty member Tony Teixeira
got Lawrence Berk's approval for the course, after which Aldrich and Teixeira put together a one-semester survey of the business and art of songwriting. Teixeira, one of the college's most colorful and well-liked teachers, also founded the first college-level course
in jingle writing at Berklee in 1969 and wrote *Music to Sell By: The Craft of Jingle Writing,*
one of the first textbooks on the musical aspects of composing for commercials.

Why should it be

We must go but we're not free.

Always looking for

What we lost tonight.

   Good life to you.

"The first semester there was only one section of the pop songwriting course, and there
were maybe 10 students," Aldrich remembers. "But we doubled enrollment the next
semester, just by word of mouth, and each semester it got bigger and bigger." A studio
course was added in 1976. Faculty member Pat Pattison developed an English elective
in the Analysis of Song Lyrics that complemented the composition electives, completing
the foundation for the Songwriting major that finally emerged in 1986.

All my dreams,

All my love,

All my life

I'll waste away

Living just for you

141

Lennie Johnson performing
with Herb Pomeroy and bassist
Major Holley in 1970.

Pianist Jaki Byard participated in the memorial to the late trumpeter and Berklee instructor Lennie Johnson.

Trumpeter Clark Terry plays with Herb Pomeroy's Concert Jazz Orchestra in the concert honoring Lennie Johnson.

A memorial concert for faculty trumpeter Lennie Johnson on March 5, 1974, was the major concert event of the 1973-74 school year. Johnson, a faculty member since 1968, died suddenly on October 7, 1973, at the age of 49. Andy McGhee, one of Johnson's closest friends on the faculty, took the lead in organizing the memorial concert. Special guests, trumpeter Clark Terry and pianist Jaki Byard, donated their services for the concert and joined faculty and student ensembles in a benefit for the Lennie Johnson Memorial Scholarship fund.

A great favorite with students, Johnson "had no real academic training, but he knew how to talk to people, how to relate," according to Charles Chapman, a former student of Johnson's. "He wanted you to learn." A trumpeter with Duke Ellington, Count Basie, and Quincy Jones, Johnson "was a great lead trumpet player and a great jazz player, and you rarely find that in one person," says Herb Pomeroy. "He was the heart and soul of my professional big band for many years."

1975	Miles Davis records *Agharta* and *Pangaea*, then goes into retirement.	Keith Jarrett records *Koln Concert*.	Pat Metheny records debut album *Bright Size Life*.	Anthony Braxton quartet records *Montreux/Berlin Concerts*.	John McLaughlin records *Shakti* with Indian musicians.
1975	Van McCoy's hit "The Hustle" sparks a dance craze.	Bruce Springsteen releases *Born to Run* and makes the covers of *Time* and *Newsweek*.	The Average White Band releases gold #1 hit single "Pick Up the Pieces."	Horn-heavy dance bands popular as Earth, Wind, and Fire releases *That's the Way of the World*, and K.C. and the Sunshine Band releases debut album.	
	1975	David A. Luce introduces the Polymoog, a completely polyphonic, velocity-sensitive instrument developed for Moog Music.			

Singer Tony Bennett proudly displays
his honorary degree.

Current Chair of the Ensemble Department Orville Wright (far left, back to camera), then a student, performs with a synthesizer quartet at the 1974 Commencement concert.

In May 1974, Tony Bennett became the first singer to receive an honorary doctorate from Berklee. The late jazz critic and scholar Leonard Feather delivered the Commencement address.

The Commencement concert, which followed immediately after the graduation exercises, featured a synthesizer quartet with faculty supervisor Michael Rendish and student Orville Wright '74, who later became chair of the Ensemble Department.

Faculty trumpeter Greg Hopkins solos with the Berklee Jazz-Rock Ensemble, conducted by Rob Rose (right), at a 1976 concert.

Starting in the fall of 1974, Berklee offered its first official Jazz-Rock Ensemble. Rob Rose '72, then a faculty member teaching arranging, theory, and ensemble, first proposed the idea. "There were a lot of good rock musicians around the school," Rose says, "so I went to Larry Berk with the idea, and he approved it. Actually, I wanted to call it the Berklee Rock Ensemble, but at that time, we couldn't get too far removed from jazz, so we called it the Jazz-Rock Ensemble.

"I really don't think it's so surprising Larry recognized the merit of the idea," Rose continues. "He started out by seeing a need and wanting to fill it, and if you could make a case for something new to him, he'd let you do it. I think that's part of his talent. He had a real knack for recognizing ability and letting people use their abilities."

Rose joined the faculty in 1972 and succeeded Larry Monroe as chair of the Performance Studies Department in 1985. He has also been in charge of summer programs since 1985. As department chair, and as founder and executive director of the faculty concert production group, the Yo Team, Rose has played an important role in the development of a curriculum for popular music performance at Berklee. In 1993, he became assistant to performance division chair for the Berklee Performance Center and on-campus summer programs.

Rob Rose conducting the Berklee Jazz-Rock Ensemble in 1975.

1976	Dexter Gordon returns to the U.S. from Europe.	Woody Herman records the 40th Anniversary Carnegie Hall Concert.	Keith Jarrett records the 10-album *Sun Bear Concerts*.	George Benson's *Breezin'* album goes platinum.	David Murray records *Flowers for Albert*.
		1976 Peter Frampton releases *Frampton Comes Alive*.	Queen releases *A Night at the Opera*.	Stevie Wonder releases *Songs in the Key of Life*.	
1976	3M and Soundstream introduce digital multitrack tape recorders.	ARP Instruments introduces Avatar, an early guitar synthesizer.	Laser lights are first used by the Who during a concert.		

In December 1974, the jazz-rock instrumental and vocal ensembles, under the direction of Rob Rose and Brian O'Connell, presented their first concert, featuring student compositions and arrangements. Instrumental Performance Department Chair John LaPorta was special guest soloist.

Trombonist and composer-in-residence Mike Gibbs.

Mike Gibbs (center, playing trombone) is known for his imaginative orchestrations, such as this combination of trombones, guitar, and violin. Comparing Gibbs to another great jazz arranger, Gary Burton says, "He is a true successor to Gil Evans."

The Only Chrome-Waterfall Orchestra

Trombonist and composer Mike Gibbs returned in 1974 as the college's first composer-in-residence and in May 1975, the Mike Gibbs Only Chrome Waterfall Orchestra gave its first concert. After leaving Berklee more than 10 years earlier, Gibbs moved to Great Britain and worked in the jazz big bands of Graham Collier, John Dankworth, and Tubby Hayes, and in film and radio. During his nearly 10 years on the Berklee faculty, Gibbs would consistently challenge his ensembles with some of the most innovative big band music of the time. Gibbs left in 1983 to further pursue his career in jazz and film composition.

Berklee composer-in-residence Mike Gibbs (left) was one of the first faculty members to consistently use student string players in his ensembles. Cellist Hank Roberts '78 (far right) was later a member of the Bill Frisell quartet.

Faculty pianist James Williams accompanies legendary jazz bassist Charles Mingus in an April 1975 clinic.

Vibraphonist Milt Jackson answers
questions at his April 1975 clinic.

Two of the biggest names in jazz conducted clinics at Berklee in spring 1975. During April, bassist Charles Mingus, in town for a concert at Symphony Hall, played duets with faculty pianist James Williams and answered questions from a capacity student audience. The next day, vibraphonist Milt Jackson, who was a special guest of the Mingus Quintet at Symphony Hall, also conducted a clinic. A graduate of Memphis State University, pianist Williams taught at Berklee from 1974 to 1977, when he joined Art Blakey's Jazz Messengers. After leaving the Messengers in 1981, Williams led his own groups, which often included faculty tenor saxophonist Bill Pierce.

Joe Hostetter recording the 1975 Commencement concert.

With the encouragement of Arif Mardin, faculty member Joe Hostetter helped install a new 8-track recording studio in the Massachusetts Avenue building in 1974. Hostetter began teaching full-time at Berklee in 1968 and helped install the first recording facilities at the college—a 2-track studio created in two adjacent basement practice rooms at 1140 Boylston Street. He also taught the college's first elective in Audio Recording in 1972, building some of the college's audio equipment himself. Hostetter's pioneering courses at Berklee laid the foundation for the Audio Recording major which he chaired from its creation in 1980 until 1983.

Joe Hostetter in the new 8-track studio at 150 Massachusetts Avenue in 1974.

Lawrence Berk, Mabel Mercer, Leonard Feist, Alma Berk, and Lee Eliot Berk at the 1975 Commencement.

Pat Metheny's guitar ensemble included (left to right) Mike Stern, Jay Azolina, and Mitch Coodley.

At the 1975 Commencement, singer Mabel Mercer became the first woman to receive an honorary degree from Berklee. After moving to the United States from her native England in 1938, Mercer's singing influenced many performers, notably Frank Sinatra, Billie Holiday, and Tony Bennett, and inspired songwriters such as Cole Porter and Alec Wilder. Music publisher Leonard Feist emphasized "the necessity of elitism, without which music would stand still and stagnate," in his Commencement address.

One of the groups featured at the Commencement concert was Pat Metheny's guitar ensemble with Mike Stern, Jay Azolina, and Mitch Coodley. Stern left Berklee to play with Blood, Sweat, and Tears. He then worked with drummer Billy Cobham before Miles Davis asked him to join his comeback band in 1981. Since leaving Davis, Stern has embarked on a successful solo career. Azolina was later guitarist in the pop-jazz group Spyro Gyra.

Don Wilkins with the new flat-bed Moviola in 1976.

Composition major Don Wilkins, later chair of the Film Scoring Department, goes over a piece with Composition Department Chair Bill Maloof.

Don Wilkins '70 joined the faculty in 1975 to teach film scoring. Berklee offered its first film scoring course, a composition seminar in the principles of dramatic program music, which covered both radio and film scores, in 1959. In 1969, Kendall Capps, a Berklee alumnus with many years of Hollywood experience, returned to build the curriculum. In 1972, Steven Gould, another Berklee alumnus with film credits, took over the program, established the first film scoring lab, and equipped it with a new editing table, synchronizer/counter, and viewer.

After Wilkins joined the faculty, he continued expanding the department and curriculum, adding courses in music editing and the history of film music, expanding the department's faculty, and upgrading equipment. In 1976, the film scoring lab acquired its first flat-bed Moviola, a machine used to synchronize sound and film. Wilkins also instituted the Berklee Film Festival in October 1977 to showcase films with scores written, produced, and performed by Berklee students. He was promoted to chair the Film Scoring major which was created in 1980.

1977 Chuck Mangione's "Feels So Good" leads *Billboard*'s top 40.

George Benson records *Weekend in L.A.*

1977 Elvis Presley dies.

Fleetwood Mac release *Rumours*.

The Eagles release *Hotel California*.

Elvis Costello releases *My Aim Is True*.

The Sex Pistols release *Never Mind the Bollocks, Here's the Sex Pistols*.

The interior of the Fenway Theatre as renovations begin.

When Lawrence Berk purchased the former Hotel Bostonian at 1140 Boylston Street in 1965, he expected that it would adequately house the college for many years to come. But as enrollment swelled from 584 in 1966 to 1,707 in 1972, the 80,000 square-foot building could not meet the college's space and facility needs, chief among them the need for a concert hall. Without a major concert hall, the college had to rent facilities such as New England Life Hall and John Hancock Hall, with all the ongoing rehearsal and logistical difficulties, for commencements and significant concerts.

So when the Bryant and Stratton School offered the former Sherry Biltmore Hotel at 150 Massachusetts Avenue and the adjoining Fenway Theatre for sale in 1972, the Berklee administration and the Board of Trustees looked at the opportunity to acquire the property with a mixture of hope and anxiety. Purchase of the 240,000 square-foot hotel and the 37,500 square-foot theater at one stroke solved many of the college's emerging space needs, but the financial challenges were daunting ones. Berklee was still absorbing the financial impact of its move from Newbury Street only six years before. The endowment was still quite small. Renovation of the new properties and 1140 Boylston Street would be an additional capital cost. To help lift the financial burden of the project, Vice President Lee Eliot Berk steered the college through its first public bond issuance, the Berklee College of Music Series A Bonds, a $6,750,000 offering with most of the interest cost subsidized by the federal government. It was the first time that Berklee entered the financial marketplace, and acceptance by the financial world was an important milestone along the road to becoming an established member of the educational community. As time went on, the college increasingly relied on tax-exempt public bond issues to meet its growing needs.

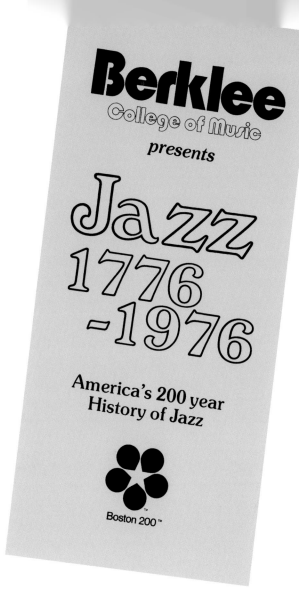

The faculty orchestra's special bicentennial concert at the opening of the Berklee Performance Center illustrated "how jazz, the American art form, reflects our heritage of ethnic diversity," according to the program book.

The marvelous 1915 movie palace, created by theater designer Thomas Lamb, was completely modernized, the stage was enlarged and an acoustic ceiling installed. Recording studios, and ensemble and rehearsals studios were built below stage level. The handsome terra cotta exterior was cleaned and restored. Next door, the 150 Massachusetts Avenue building was used to house classrooms, an expanded library, practice rooms, and a major residence hall.

The renovated theater was rechristened the Berklee Performance Center and grand opening ceremonies took place on April 5, 1976. In his dedication address, Massachusetts Governor Michael Dukakis called the new 1,227-seat facility "an out-standing contribution to the cultural resources of the city and state." The 17-piece Berklee All-Star Jazz Faculty Orchestra, under the direction of Tony Teixeira, performed "Jazz 1776-1976," a 200-year history of American music composed and arranged by Teixeira, Ted Pease, and Larry Monroe, with narration by Monroe and Ray Copeland. Trumpeter Copeland, a veteran of the bands of Thelonious Monk, Art Blakey, and other jazz greats, taught at Berklee from 1976 to 1979. His son, Keith, is a 1973 alumnus and also a former faculty member.

Since 1976, as Berklee courses and majors diversified, the Performance Center has provided a laboratory for student performers, producers, and recording engineers. "We see the Performance Center as a giant classroom where people can learn about performing and the technical side of presenting a show," says Rob Rose.

Student Jamie Glaser '77 appeared with his band
Yarbles at an early Performance Center concert.

College-affiliated ensembles began appearing at the Berklee Performance Center even
before the grand opening. Among the first groups to appear was a percussion ensemble
directed by Dean Anderson and featuring faculty guest Gary Burton. Student guitarist Bill
Frisell '77, who became one of the most in-demand jazz guitarists in New York, also performed with the percussionists. In addition to appearing with Paul Motian, John Zorn,
and many others in the 1980s and 1990s, Frisell led his own groups which featured
Berklee classmates, bassist Kermit Driscoll '78 and cellist Hank Roberts.

Among the first student ensembles to appear at the Performance Center were Shel
Sondheim's Catharsis. Ictus, a synthesizer ensemble led by David Mash '76, who later
became assistant dean of curriculum for academic technology, also made a spring appearance. Guitarist Jamie Glaser '77, who later toured and recorded with Jean Luc Ponty and
became a successful Los Angeles player, performed with his group Yarbles in March.

"At first, I had to recruit concerts—first faculty, then scheduled ensembles, then student
concerts," Larry Monroe remembers. "To make sure there was a faculty presence, I
emceed every concert between 1978 and 1988. Pretty soon we were drowning in concerts and we added staff people. Today, between the Performance Center and the small-
er recital halls, we do 24 concerts a week."

One of the most in-demand guitarists at Berklee while he was a student,
Bill Frisell performed in a 1976 percussion ensemble concert.

Trumpeter Thad Jones, Lawrence Berk, George
Wein, John Hammond, drummer Mel Lewis, and
Lee Eliot Berk, at the 1976 Commencement. Jones
and Lewis were invited to Commencement as
guests of the Berks.

Berklee honored jazz impresario George Wein with an honorary degree in 1976. Wein,
founder of the Newport Jazz Festival, said in his acceptance speech, "Nobody can stop
the force of jazz. It cannot be ignored. People who play jazz are the greatest musicians
in the world." Record producer John Hammond delivered the Commencement address.
Hammond—who produced important early recordings by the Fletcher Henderson and
Count Basie big bands, clarinetist Benny Goodman, and singer Billie Holiday, and signed
Bob Dylan and Bruce Springsteen to their first major label contracts—praised Wein for
initiating a social as well as musical revolution. "He not only started jazz festivals, he also
initiated a social revolution; for at that time all racial discrimination in hotel accommo-
dations were ordered stopped in Newport."

Although classical vocal training was widely available at the college level, there were no programs in the vocal styles that continued to emerge and play a dominant role in contemporary American music. Berklee moved to fill the void in college-level contemporary vocal education and in 1978, Berklee students were allowed to declare voice as their principal instrument for the first time.

A small number of voice students attended the college from the time it was founded. Lennie Lane supervised vocal instruction at Schillinger House and coached Berklee voice students until the early 1970s. Vocal courses for Music Education majors were also offered for many years. But interest in a program in contemporary singing styles did not start to grow stronger until the early 1970s. In 1976, Charles Cassey was appointed director of vocal activity, and began to build a program for singers.

Brian O'Connell took over as founding chair of the Voice Department in 1978 and laid the foundation on which the department continues to build. A fine choral director, O'Connell believed it was important to expose students to choral masterworks in addition to offering training in contemporary jazz and popular styles. He led the Berklee Concert Choir unti his departure from the college in 1984.

Lennie Lane (right), who started teaching voice at Schillinger House in the 1940s, was the only voice teacher at Berklee for many years.

1978 Herbie Hancock and Chick Corea record jazz piano duets.	Art Ensemble of Chicago records *Nice Guys.*	Cecil Taylor Unit records *Three Phasis.*	
1978 The disco soundtrack to *Saturday Night Fever* is released.	The Cars release their debut.	Hard rock band Van Halen release their self-titled debut.	Parliament/Funkadelic release *One Nation Under a Groove.* Billy Joel releases *52nd Street.*
	1978 Dave Smith of Sequential Circuit develops the first microprocessor in a synthesizer, the Prophet 5.		

Current Voice Department faculty member
Mili Bermejo '89 performing as a student.

Brian O'Connell directs the Berklee Concert Choir.

In 1976, there were 30 vocalists at Berklee. Ten years later, there were 303 students who declared voice as their principal instrument. The tenfold increase in singers had a dramatic impact on the college. Voice students further widened the stylistic range covered at the college. Berklee initially focused on the instrumental craft, arranging, and composition skills demanded in jazz and other contemporary instrumental music, widening its scope with the inclusion of electric guitar, which brought rock and pop music into the school. Because contemporary vocal music encompasses an even broader range of styles, voice students drove the move to rock and pop music to an even greater extent than guitar. And because singers require backup bands, ensembles were created in more styles.

Besides broadening the curriculum, rock and pop vocalists established a new standard of showmanship at Berklee concerts. Elaborate stage presentations such as Country Night and the Singers' Showcase are a direct result of the performance requirements of pop and rock singing styles.

The Jazz Choir in concert at the Berklee Performance Center.

161

Woody Herman holding the honorary degree he received in 1977.

With their tribute to Woody Herman, John LaPorta (right, playing clarinet) and a student ensemble initiated the Commencement concert practice of performing the music of the honorary degree recipient.

A wheelchair-bound Woody Herman, visibly moved by the standing ovation that greeted him, received his honorary degree from Berklee in 1977. Injured in an automobile accident in March, Herman swore to President Lawrence Berk that he would attend the ceremony "if I have to be carried in on a stretcher."

Herman flew into Boston a day early to attend the Commencement concert, which inaugurated a Berklee tradition of performing a musical tribute to the honorary degree recipient (or recipients) each year. John LaPorta conducted a student ensemble in several classic Herman charts, including "Woodchopper's Ball" and "Bijou." LaPorta, a former Herman sideman, also wrote a piece especially for the occasion, "One Man Jazz Journey, or 'Whatever Happened to the Golden Wedding Gang.' "

Paul Schmeling.

In March 1995, Paul Schmeling
directed and emceed a faculty concert,
"50 Years of Jazz Piano."

In 1977, Paul Schmeling was appointed chair of the Piano Department. A faculty member since 1961, Schmeling had chaired both the Ear Training and the Piano departments since 1974. When responsibilities for both departments grew too large for one person to handle, Larry Monroe was promoted to chair of Ear Training and Schmeling retained the Piano Department. A Boston Conservatory graduate, Schmeling has administered the growth of the department's facilities, curriculum, and faculty. Building on the department's solid foundation in jazz, new courses have kept pace with new developments in jazz, rock, and popular music. Piano labs were established and, in the 1980s, private studios were equipped to incorporate synthesizers and MIDI. The new technologies could simulate different playing situations—from small ensemble to big band—to improve the effectiveness of practicing and teaching. In 1989, expanded piano practice facilities were created at 171A Massachusetts Avenue.

Singers perform at the Jazz-Rock Ensemble tribute to Motown Records.

Bassist Slam Stewart (right), famous for singing in harmony with his bop wing, appeared with Phil Wilson (left) and the Dues Band in March 1979.

By the 1978 academic year, a greater variety of music was heard at Berklee than ever before. In November, the Jazz-Rock Ensemble's "Takin' Care of Business III" concert, "A Tribute to Motown," was the group's second theme concert dedicated entirely to the music of one style or performer. In their first theme concert the previous semester, the ensemble paid tribute to the Beatles.

In March 1979, drummer Tommy Campbell '79 assembled a jazz-funk quartet ("with the emphasis on funk," the concert program said) featuring guitarist Kevin Eubanks '79. Eubanks would be familiar to millions of television viewers as the guitarist in the "Tonight Show" Band of Branford Marsalis, another Berklee alumnus. Eubanks became leader of the band in 1995.

If jazz was no longer the only focus of activity at Berklee, it still played a leading role at the college. In March 1979, legendary swing-era bassist Slam Stewart appeared with Phil Wilson and the International Dues Band in a concert that included "Slambitious," a composition written especially for the concert, and an arrangement of Duke Ellington's "Mood Indigo."

Kevin Eubanks (right) as a student in 1979.

	1979 Charles Mingus and Stan Kenton die.	Spyro Gyra's single "Morning Dance" goes gold.	Pat Metheny records *American Garage*.
1979 The No Nukes benefit concert is held.	The Police meld reggae and new wave rock on their debut U.S. hit "Roxanne."	The Clash release *London Calling*.	Disco diva Donna Summer goes rock with platinum hits "Hot Stuff" and "Bad Girls."
	1979 Denon custom digital recorders available.	Digital recording on video tape offered by Nakamichi, Sony F-1, JVC Pro.	

Dean Anderson rehearses the Berklee Percussion Ensemble.

Dean Anderson became chair of the Percussion Department in 1979, replacing Gary Chaffee. A New England Conservatory of Music graduate who has performed and recorded with the Boston Symphony Orchestra, Boston Opera Company, and Boston Musica Viva, Anderson joined the faculty in 1974. As chair, he has overseen marked growth in the faculty and curriculum of the department. With the addition of the first college-level courses in hand percussion in 1988, the department offers four principal instrument options: drum set, vibraphone, percussion, and hand percussion. Forty elective labs covering a wide range of contemporary styles, including electronic percussion, Latin percussion, and orchestral techniques, make Berklee's program one of the most comprehensive in the world. The annual department-sponsored "Percussion Unlimited" concert given each year by the Berklee Percussion Ensemble, under Anderson's direction, has featured visiting artists such as drummer Peter Erskine, vibraphonist Dave Samuels, saxophonist Dave Liebman, and vibraphonist Gary Burton.

Faculty percussionists (left to right) Giovanni Hidalgo, Ed Uribe '82, Victor Mendoza, and Sa Davis with Dean Anderson.

Jack DeJohnette records *Special Edition*.

Betty Carter records *The Audience with Betty Carter*.

Blondie releases "Heart of Glass."

The Doobie Brothers release *Minute by Minute*.

Pink Floyd releases *The Wall*.

The Talking Heads release *Fear of Music*.

Sony 1610 offers digital recording on 3/4 inch video tape.

Digital multitracks marketed by Sony, Mitsubishi, and Studer.

Lawrence Berk accepts his honorary degree from James G. Zafris, Jr., Chair of the Board of Trustees.

Pianist Teddy Wilson performs with faculty member Tony Teixeira on bass and Wilson's son Steve Wilson '82 on drums.

Teddy Wilson (front row, right) acknowledges the audience's applause after receiving his honorary degree.

Pianist Teddy Wilson received an honorary degree at the 1979 Commencement. In the late 1930s, Wilson backed singer Billie Holiday on many of her important early recordings and helped break racial barriers with the Benny Goodman Trio, one of the first racially integrated big-name jazz groups.

The 1979 Commencement was the first at which more than one honorary degree was conferred. President Lawrence Berk, who had submitted his resignation to the Board of Trustees on December 5, 1978, also received an honorary degree of doctor of music education. It was a fitting gesture from the school he had built from a small number of private students in a Back Bay studio to a fully accredited college of music with an enrollment of over 2,500 students from 66 countries—the largest independent college of music in the world.

Two generations of the Berk family at the 1979 Commencement: Alma (left) and Lawrence (holding degree) with Lee Eliot (second from left) and his wife Susan G. Berk (right).

Rob Rose directs a Commencement
concert rehearsal.

Chapter Five

Berklee College of Music
1979 – 1985

Lawrence Berk's retirement confronted the members of the Board of Trustees with their first major leadership decision. Since internal recruitment of faculty and staff was largely responsible for the college's success up to that time, the board felt Berk's successor should come from within the college community. Internal candidates, it was felt, were best equipped to understand Berklee's unique strengths and could maintain educational continuity and momentum as the college faced the challenges that lay ahead. In June 1979, the board elected Vice President Lee Eliot Berk, son of founder Lawrence Berk, as the next president of Berklee College of Music. At the same time, they appointed Administrator Robert Share to the additional position of provost to better reflect his responsibilities at the college.

Under the leadership of President Lee Eliot Berk, the college would undergo significant academic and administrative change and growth. Well-established courses in film scoring, electronic music, audio recording, and jazz composition and arranging were organized into new majors. The college became a leader in the educational applications and use of music technology. It also underwent significant administrative reorganization. Several new deans were hired and a new division structure more appropriately organized management of the curriculum. Berklee's essential educational mission remained intact, and the management changes more effectively helped prepare students for a rapidly changing music industry.

1980 David Murray Octet records *Ming.*

Pat Metheny records *As Falls Wichita, So Falls Wichita Falls.*

Wynton Marsalis joins Art Blakey's Jazz Messengers; releases debut album.

1980 John Lennon is shot and killed in New York.

The B-52's quirky self-titled debut goes gold.

Talking Heads release *Remain in Light.*

The Pretenders release their self-titled debut album.

Drummer John Bonham dies, Led Zeppelin breaks up.

1980 Development of sampling technology.

Roger Linn introduces the LM-1, the first programmable drum machine to feature digitally sampled sounds.

Lawrence Bethune in his office, just after he was appointed dean of students.

Bethune with students: "I feel we should listen to what students have to say about Berklee," he says. "I was always big into the student voice."

Lawrence Bethune '71 was appointed dean of students in the fall of 1979, after Dean Gerald Siddons departed. A faculty member since 1971, Bethune had also served as one of six unit counselors (an early student counseling service), and supervised the Student Tutorial Program and the Listening Lab. In 1978, he had been appointed chair of the Ear Training Department.

Changes in the student population necessitated the upgrading of student services originally created under Dean Siddons, and increased responsibilities for the dean of students. "Slowly but surely, the college was changing as the student population got younger," Bethune observes. "They were no long primarily pros coming in off the road to build their skills. Most of the students were just out of high school, liked music, and wanted to go to college. So, the Office of the Dean of Students had to offer programs for this new kind of Berklee student."

The expanded Office of the Dean of Students evolved to oversee all nonacademic aspects of student life at Berklee. These include admissions, financial aid, counseling, registration, housing, and other student services, activities, events, and clubs. Since 1981, a host of Berklee employees have contributed to the growth and efficient operation of these various offices. Under Larry Bethune's leadership, the Office of the Dean of Students has grown to encompasss the growing needs of an international student community with changing musical, educational, and developmental experiences.

From 1967 to 1984, the college's registrar was Dave Matayabas. Matayabas taught bass at Berklee from 1961 to 1967, and was promoted to director of payroll/personnel systems in 1990. He retired in 1995. Russell Lombardi replaced Matayabas and served until 1987, when Phil Morimoto '83 took over the job. Lynn King replaced Morimoto in 1995. Management of the college's dormitories has been in the hands of William Mackay since 1983. The Counseling Center opened in 1982; Jeff Callahan was the founding director of counseling.

In 1978, Larry Bethune, then chair of the Ear Training Department, conducts a vocal ensemble recording session.

Drummer Buddy Rich performs with the International Dues Band at the 1980 Commencement concert.

Buddy Rich, President Lee Eliot Berk, and John Williams.

Academy Award-winning film composer John Williams, then recently appointed conductor and musical director of the Boston Pops Orchestra, and jazz drummer Buddy Rich received honorary degrees at the 1980 Commencement ceremony. *Billboard* Publications Senior Vice President Mort Nasatir delivered the Commencement address.

The Commencement concert on the previous night featured the film music of John Williams performed by Phil Wilson and the International Dues Band. The evening concluded with a surprise performance of Phil Wilson's Grammy-nominated arrangement of "Mercy, Mercy, Mercy" with drummer Rich sitting in.

Don Wilkins (standing, far right) explains the working of a flat-bed Moviola to a group of students.

Several new majors were added to the Berklee curriculum for the 1980-81 academic year—Film Scoring, Electronic Music, Audio Recording, and Jazz Composition and Arranging.

Faculty member Don Wilkins was appointed chair of the new Film Scoring program. Under the leadership of Wilkins, the department continuously monitored film industry technologies and incorporated them into the Berklee environment. In 1985, synthesizers and MIDI were introduced into film scoring labs and ProTools was in use in 1993. A course in Digital Video was offered in 1994. "We are driven by where the career opportunities lie, that's our charge and our mission," Wilkins says. "What we have in terms of facilities is a direct result of observing techniques being used in the industry."

Don Wilkins stands at the television set as composer John Williams (at far left, pointing) discusses his score to *Jaws* during a 1981 visit.

Ted Pease at the drums with a faculty big band which he codirected with Larry Monroe.

Faculty members Robin Coxe-Yeldham (far left) and Joe Hostetter (second from left) join Arif Mardin (second from right) with his engineer before presenting a lecture to students on production techniques.

Other faculty members were promoted to head newly created departments. Michael Rendish, who had taught the first electronic music course at Berklee, and supervised the development of the curriculum, chaired the Electronic Music Department. Ted Pease remained as chair of the Arranging Department, and a new Jazz Composition and Arranging major was offered. Joe Hostetter was picked to chair the Audio Recording Department.

Michael Rendish gives a synthesizer demonstration in 1979.

Fred Schmidt (left) leads
an in-class discussion.

Faculty member Fred Schmidt began the fall 1980 semester as chair of the General Music Department. A professional trombonist, Schmidt earned a M.Ed. from Cambridge College and started teaching theory, music education, and ensemble courses at Berklee in 1972. In 1986, he became founding chair of the Professional Music Department. Working closely with departmental advisors, students majoring in Professional Music design an individual educational plan for course work leading to mastery of an area of concentration they select. As chair of the department, Schmidt has worked to ensure the curriculum remains relevant to contemporary music industry demands.

1981 Old and New Dreams releases
Playing.

Muhal Richard Abrams records *Blues Forever.*

Styx releases best-selling *Paradise Theater.*

Rush releases *Moving Pictures.*

Sheena Easton releases debut single
"Morning Train."

The Go-Go's debut with "Our Lips Are
Sealed."

John Lennon and Yoko Ono's *Double Fantasy*
goes platinum.

Nineteen-year-old Terri Lyne Carrington with Thornebird at a concert in November 1980.

Victor Vanacore '74, Barry Manilow's musical director (left), and faculty member Jon Aldrich (center), laugh at Manilow's answer to a question from the audience at his 1980 clinic.

Concerts and clinics during the 1980-81 academic year and in the summer of 1981 included some notable "firsts." Singer/songwriter Barry Manilow was the first pop music superstar to visit the college for a clinic. Attendance at his appearance reflected the growing interest of Berklee students in songwriting.

The college's first official gospel group, the Reverence Gospel Choir, made its first concert appearance in July 1981. The choir appeared on a bill with Thornebird, an all-female student ensemble led by trumpeter Edwina Thorne '81. The group, which included drummer Terri Lyne Carrington '83, was evidence of the increasing presence of female students at the school. A musical prodigy, Carrington was offered a scholarship to Berklee when she was 11. She was the house drummer on the "Arsenio Hall Show" and recorded as a leader and with Wayne Shorter, Al Jarreau, and others.

The Reverence Gospel Choir performed gospel music and jazz during their concert with Thornebird.

Dean Richard Bobbitt, pianist Billy
Taylor, and President Lee Eliot Berk.

Pianist Billy Taylor and producer John Hammond received honorary degrees at the 1981
Commencement. Pianist and educator Taylor previously spoke at Berklee's 25th anniversary graduation in 1970. Pioneering jazz record producer John Hammond, who delivered
the 1976 Commencement address, was absent due to an illness in his family, and
received his degree in absentia.

1982 Rap gains greater visibility with release of *The Message* by Grandmaster Flash and the Furious Five, and *8th Wonder* by the Sugarhill Gang.	Techno-pop bands such as A Flock of Seagulls become popular.	The Stray Cats revive rockabilly on their album *Built for Speed*.	Prince tops the dance charts with his hit "Little Red Corvette."
1982 Compact disc recordings introduced.	Dave Smith and others collaborate to define MIDI.	Raymond Kurzweil introduces the Kurzweil 250, and Yamaha introduces the DX7.	

In a surprise ceremony at the end of a Berklee Performance Center concert in November 1981, President Lee Eliot Berk conferred an honorary degree on Count Basie, whose Kansas City riff-based swing was one of the most popular and influential styles to emerge in the 1930s. Singer Tony Bennett, who made two popular albums with the Count Basie Orchestra, performed with the band at the November 1981 concert.

Count Basie swings and Tony Bennett sings at the Berklee Performance Center in 1981.

1982 Charlie Haden's Liberation Music   Thelonious Monk dies.
Orchestra records *Ballad of the Fallen*.

Toto wins seven Grammys for *Toto IV*.   Elvis Costello releases *Imperial Bedroom*.   Duran Duran debuts with   Culture Club debuts with   The J. Geils Band releases *Dare*.
"Hungry Like a Wolf."   "Do You Really Want to Hurt Me?"

President Lee Eliot Berk presents Donald Harrison with the 1981 Lennie Johnson Award.

Greg Osby (right) solos with Phil Wilson and the International Dues Band during a December 1981 concert.

The instrumental jazz groups that were the historic foundation of the college continued to prosper. Phil Wilson's International Dues Band featured alto saxophonist Greg Osby '83. After leaving Berklee, Osby recorded with the Brooklyn M-Base groups that explored innovative fusions of jazz with funk and hip-hop. Elsewhere, saxophonist Donald Harrison '83 led a quartet featuring Jeff Watts '81 on drums. Harrison later joined Art Blakey and the Jazz Messengers, then led a quintet with trumpeter Terence Blanchard, before recording albums as a leader and as a sideman with Latin pianist Eddie Palmieri and drummer Roy Haynes. Watts became a regular member of bands led by his fellow Berklee student, saxophonist Branford Marsalis '80.

President Lee Eliot Berk (left) congratulates David Friend upon his election to the Board of Trustees.

In the early 1980s, the Board of Trustees added several new members and grew increasingly active,.as the college met new challenges. In September 1981, two new members were elected: Boston Pops Associate Director Harry Ellis Dickson and David Friend, Technical Director of Computer Picture Corporation and cofounder of electronic musical instrument manufacturer ARP Instruments. Several months before, in April 1980, attorney Herbert Baer was elected to the board. In February 1981, educational consultant and saxophonist Irving Schwartz, who was also Social Studies Department chair at Brookline High School, joined the board.

President Berk welcomes Harry Ellis Dickson to the Board of Trustees.

Matt Glaser (center stage, front) leads a string lab.

Randy Sabien.

Violinist Matt Glaser was hired in 1981 to create a more comprehensive String Department. Violin was taught at the school throughout its history, and in 1979, violinist Randel Sabien '77, founding chair of the String Department, began teaching and developing a more formalized string curriculum. But Glaser was charged with building a faculty, creating a coherent and more comprehensive program, and fully integrating string players into the general educational framework of the college. "Strings, along with guitar and voice, is an area in which the college has really blazed a trail that isn't followed anywhere else," says Glaser. "Berklee has the only collegiate string department anywhere that is not idiomatically restrictive. You have technical requirements that you must pass to master your instrument, but we do not demand at anytime that a student play any particular idiom—classical, jazz, or any other style."

Robert Lacey, Chair of the
Music Education Department
from 1974 to 1981.

Hosted by Music Education Department Chair John Hagon (second from left),
visting lecturer Karl Bruhn (center) hold a seminar on advocacy for school music.

In 1981, faculty member John Hagon succeeded Robert Lacey as chair of the Music Education Department. Dr. Lacey, who earned his Ed.D. from Boston University, joined the Berklee Music Education faculty in 1971. He became chair in 1974, building the department into the largest college music education department in Massachusetts. Under his leadership, the department became the first music education program in the state to join the Interstate Certification Compact, qualifying graduates of the Berklee program for reciprocal teacher certification in 32 other states. While Lacey was chair, the department also established a resource center in 1975 and expanded its innovative program of summer music educator workshops.

Hagon, who received his M.M. from Boston University, joined the faculty in 1978 and taught conducting, scoring, and music education courses. Under Hagon's leadership, the Music Education Department revised its curriculum to provide a more flexible program of study leading to one of three different types of teacher certification. New courses were established focusing on important contemporary issues in education, including Advocacy for Public School Music, Mainstreaming, and Computer Applications in Music Education. The department also became a leader in training students in the application of new music education technologies.

183

The Counseling Center opened its doors in 1982.

In 1982, the Counseling Center opened, offering a varied menu of services designed to meet the needs of a changing student body. Academic advising, previously offered only to entering freshmen to help them register for classes, was now available to all students and included guidance in declaring a major and other decisions. Personal counseling was offered for the first time. Special counseling services and courses in English as a Second Language were made available to international students to help them adjust to life in the United States. Career counseling was also offered through the Counseling Center until a separate Career Resource Center opened in 1987.

1983 Henry Threadgill Sextet records *Just the Facts and Pass the Bucket.*   Branford Marsalis records *Scenes in the City.*   Keith Jarrett forms Standards trio.

1983 Michael Jackson releases *Thriller.*   Motown Records celebrates its 25th anniversary.   Madonna's self-titled debut album is released.   Lionel Ritchie releases "All Night Long."   R.E.M. releases *Murmur.*

1983 Introduction of MIDI.   Commercial use of FM synthesis technology.

At the 1982 Commencement concert, bandleader John Dankworth solos while singer Cleo Laine and faculty member Mike Gibbs (a former Dankworth trombonist) listen approvingly.

Gary Burton at the conclusion of his Commencement address.

In 1982, honorary degrees were awarded to English singer Cleo Laine and saxophonist and arranger John Dankworth. A vocalist with a four-octave range, Laine has been nominated for Grammy awards in the female popular, classical, and jazz categories. Her husband and musical director John Dankworth not only fronted an innovative big band but also wrote film and symphonic music. Gary Burton delivered the Commencement address.

Dean Richard Bobbitt, John Dankworth, Cleo Laine, and President Lee Eliot Berk.

The George Adams/Don Pullen Quartet records at the Village Vanguard.

Miles Davis records *Star People*.

Eurythmics release debut single "Sweet Dreams (Are Made of This)."

Cyndi Lauper debuts with "Girls Just Want to Have Fun."

Wham! debuts with "Bad Boys."

Men at Work go platinum with *Cargo*.

Mike Ihde takes a solo with his guitar ensemble Flat Rats and Sail Cats.

William Leavitt (left) leads the Shopping Center Seven + One, featuring faculty member Charles Chapman on bass.

In April, "Guitar Night VII" showed how the guitar ensemble had evolved to meet the musically diversified tastes and educational needs of Berklee students. Department Chair William Leavitt led the Shopping Center Seven + One in several jazz standards. Charles Chapman led the Baroque Jazz Ensemble in arrangements of Bach and Mozart. Mike Ihde '72 led the country and western-flavored Flat Rats and Sail Cats and Michael T. (Tom) Szymczak '69 led Tom's Thumbs, which played jazz-rock compositions by John Scofield, and several other arrangements.

Tom Szymczak (left) with Tom's Thumbs.

Rob Rose (second from left) with his wife Jodie Rose (left) and the original Yo Team, Nancy Tellier Morris, Ken Zambello, and Mike Morris.

The Yo Team in 1995—Rob Rose, Tom Stein (second from left), Richard Evans (center, back) and Ken Zambello—with honorary degree recipients Natalie Cole and James Taylor.

By the early 1980s, concert production was no longer a matter of putting a band on stage with a few microphones. Since the late 1970s, when faculty member Peter Hume '78 began helping Rob Rose produce Berklee Jazz-Rock Ensemble shows, concerts at the college had become increasingly ambitious. As the curriculum embraced a wider range of styles, singers and instrumentalists needed to know more about choreography and other performance skills, and student productions began to incorporate special lighting, set design, and special effects.

Starting with the 1983 Commencement concert tribute to honorary degree recipient Quincy Jones, the Yo Team, a group of faculty members from different disciplines, has worked with students to establish a high standard of performance and production quality at Berklee concerts. The first Yo Team included Rob Rose, Ken Zambello '82, Nancy Tellier Morris '80, and Mike Morris. Other team members have included Camille Schmidt '84, Greg MacPherson, Walter Beasley '84, Jackie Beard '80, and Jennifer Terry '86. The Yo Team is responsible for producing high profile events such as the Entering Student Convocation concert, Country Night, Jazz-Rock Ensemble, Singers' Showcase, International Night, and the Commencement concert. Yo Team productions have also helped to more fully integrate rock and pop vocal styles into the Berklee curriculum.

President Lee Eliot Berk, Quincy Jones, Arif Mardin, and Chancellor Lawrence Berk at the 1983 Commencement.

Singers and members of the Jazz-Rock Ensemble crowd the stage for "The Q Medley," the Ken Zambello arrangement that climaxed the 1983 Commencement concert tribute to Quincy Jones.

Makoto Ozone (left) and Keiichi Ishibashi '83 provide a duo interlude at the 1983 Commencement concert.

Program

The Music of Quincy Jones

The Berklee Concert Jazz Orchestra
directed by Herb Pomeroy

Jessica's Day ....

Wail Bait .... *arranged by Chris Swanson*

Blues Bitter-Sweet .... *arranged by Jose Valderrama*

Stockholm Sweetnin' .... *arranged by Mike Gibbs*

An Interlude with the Makoto Ozone/Keiichi Ishibashi Duo ...... *arranged by Mike Gibbs*

Pogo Stick .... *arranged by Joe Carrier*

Intermission

The Berklee Jazz Rock Ensemble
directed by Robert E. Rose

The Dude .... *Quincy Jones*
arranged by Ken Zambello

When You're Smiling .... *Fisher/Goodwin & Shay*
arranged by Ken Zambello

Everything Must Change .... *Benard Ighner*
arranged by Ken Zambello

Smackwater Jack .... *Carole King*
arranged by Ken Zambello

Quincy T.V. Medley .... *arranged by Michael Morris*
Chump Change (from "High Rollers"), Ironside, Hickey-Burr (from "The Bill Cosby Show"), Sanford and Son, The Anderson Tapes, "Roots" Mural Theme, The End of the Yellow Brick Road (from "The Wiz")

Maybe Tomorrow .... *Quincy Jones/Lyrics by A. & M. Bergman*

Finger On The Trigger .... *Donna Summer*
arranged by Michael Morris

The Q Medley .... *arranged by Ken Zambello*
What Good Is A Song?, It's My Party, The Girl Is Mine, Beat It, Baby Come To Me, Just Once, Superstition, Give Me The Night, Off The Wall, Ease On Down The Road

In 1983, Quincy Jones received an honorary doctorate from Berklee, the school he attended in 1951 when it was called Schillinger House. Commencement speaker, producer and Senior Vice President of Atlantic Studios Arif Mardin, whom Jones had recommended for a scholarship in 1958, reminisced about his years at Berklee and his friendship with Quincy Jones. He concluded by telling the graduating class, "without rejecting the music of the past, always look to the future."

The Berklee Concert Jazz Orchestra, under the direction of Herb Pomeroy, and the Berklee Jazz-Rock Ensemble, directed by Rob Rose, played the music of Quincy Jones at the Commencement concert the evening previous to the baccalaureate ceremony. The wide-ranging program included selections from Jones' jazz, pop, and television music. The duo of Makoto Ozone and Keiichi Ishibashi shared the first half of the program with the Concert Jazz Orchestra. After graduating, Ozone had a successful jazz career, recording and performing with Gary Burton and as a leader.

Quincy Jones presents Lawrence Berk with the funds that established the
Quincy Jones Scholarship in 1958.

Eighteen-year-old Quincy Jones (left) was in Fred Berman's trumpet ensemble
when Bobby Hackett (third from left) visited Schillinger House in 1951.

Quincy Jones has enjoyed one of the most prolific and successful careers in music of any
Berklee alumnus. In the 1950s, Jones wrote and arranged for jazz musicians like Clifford
Brown, Sarah Vaughan, Dizzy Gillespie, Dinah Washington, and Ray Charles. In 1964,
Jones became the first African-American vice president of Mercury Records. Soon after-
wards he began writing music for films and television. His film scores include the
Academy Award-winning music for *In Cold Blood* (1967). He also composed the theme
music for television shows, including "Ironside" and "The Bill Cosby Show."

In 1983, Jones produced Michael Jackson's *Thriller*, the best-selling album of all time,
with seven top 10 hits. He and Jackson followed up their success with the 1987 album
Bad which included five number-one singles, more than any other album in the history
of the *Billboard* charts. In 1985, Jones produced the best-selling single "We Are the
World" featuring an all-star group including Jackson, Stevie Wonder, Bob Dylan, Ray
Charles, Bruce Springsteen, and many others. At the time of Berklee's 50th anniversary
year, 1995, Jones was still a very active producer and composer, but was branching out
into new areas. He was acquiring television properties through his company, Qwest
Broadcasting. And his multimedia coventure with Time Warner, Quincy Jones-David
Salzman Entertainment, was preparing to produce movies, TV shows, and other forms
of entertainment in all types of media.

A page from
Quincy Jones'
Schillinger System
notebook.

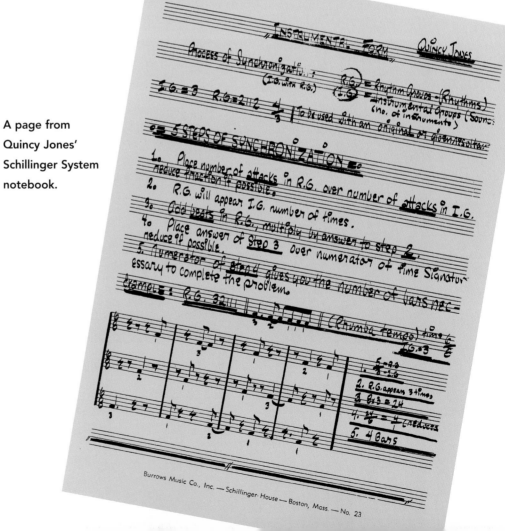

Trumpet students Quincy Jones (third to the right of conductor Fred Berman) and Herb Pomeroy (fifth to Berman's right) at the 1951 annual concert.

President Lee Eliot Berk, Don Puluse, and faculty member Wayne Wadhams in 1985 with the first *Mix* magazine TEC Award (on control board, next to Wadhams).

Don Puluse.

In August 1983, Don Puluse was hired to chair the new Music Production and Engineering Department and revise the Audio Engineering major. Building on the foundation laid by Audio Engineering Chair Joe Hostetter, Puluse added fresh courses, faculty, and established improved facilities in order to effectively merge the new major with the mission of the college. In September 1984, a second 8-track and a third 24-track studio were added, upgrading college facilities to match current industry standards, and enlarging them to accommodate more students. In November 1985, the efforts of Puluse and the department were recognized when the program won the first of its three *Mix* magazine TEC Awards for technical excellence and creativity in the field of institutional recording technology.

"We take a hands-on approach," Puluse says. "Working effectively in the recording studio environment is similar to playing an instrument; you can't learn everything just from the textbook. You can learn a lot of theory, but you have to learn the intangibles. Berklee gives you the fundamentals, *and* a lot of experience in the studio."

Before he came to Berklee, Puluse had engineered several gold and platinum records including *Chicago II, III, IV,* and *IX*; Bob Dylan's *Self Portrait*; and Sly Stone's *Stand* and *Everyday People*. He received a Grammy nomination for his engineering of Leonard Bernstein's *Mass*.

Don Puluse supervises a student recording session.

The first Berklee Singers' Showcase took place in November 1983. The idea for the concert, which featured several of Berklee's best vocalists in a broad range of styles, came from Performance Studies Chair Larry Monroe. "I noticed the vocal students weren't getting enough concert opportunities," Monroe says. "So I thought this would be a good way to find good singers and feature them. It's the ultimate classroom."

Once each semester, participating vocalists go through a rigorous audition process. The six or seven selected are then matched with student arrangers, writers, and producers to create a dynamic program that is consistently one of the most popular student concert events of the semester. The whole process, from audition to production, was developed by Rob Rose and Orville Wright. "We try to make the experience as real to life as possible," says Rob Rose.

Betty Carter and Cyrus Chestnut.

During the fall semester of the 1983-84 academic year, Betty Carter, considered by most critics to be the premier jazz vocalist of her generation, engaged in a question-and-answer session with students at the Berklee Performance Center. When Carter asked for a pianist to accompany her, students began chanting for Cyrus Chestnut '85 who joined Carter on stage for a version of "Body and Soul." Carter remembered her memorable first encounter with the young pianist and hired him for her trio in 1990. Chestnut also worked with trumpeters Wynton Marsalis and Terence Blanchard and drummer Carl Allen. His 1994 debut recording as a leader, *Revelation*, was hailed as jazz album of the year by *The Village Voice*.

1984 Count Basie dies.	Wynton Marsalis receives Grammys in jazz and classical categories.	John Zorn releases *The Big Gundown*.	Hal Wilner produces *That's the Way I Feel Now*, a tribute to Thelonious Monk.
1984 Bob Geldof organizes supergroup Band Aid.	Rap label Def Jam Record Company is formed.	Prince's *Purple Rain* soundtrack wins three Grammys and an Oscar.	Tina Turner releases her Grammy-winning *Private Dancer*.	Bruce Springsteen releases *Born in the U.S.A.*

Robert Share (second from right) and Lee Eliot Berk greet Arif Mardin (left) and Quincy Jones (right) at the 1983 Commencement.

On April 5, 1984, the entire Berklee community was shocked and saddened by news of the sudden death of Provost Robert Share at the age of 55. Share, who died of a heart attack at his desk, was a respected teacher and highly regarded administrator at Berklee for over 30 years. Chancellor Lawrence Berk said, "My wife and I have known Bob since he was 17 years old. He was like a son." Responsible for most of the daily operation of the college, Share was, according to all who knew him, a good-natured and seemingly tireless man. "In many ways he was the heart and soul of the school," says Ted Pease.

Robert Share (right) and Oscar Peterson in early 1984.

197

Bon Jovi releases debut single "Runaway."   Mötley Crüe debuts with "Looks That Kill."   Billy Ocean's single "Caribbean Queen (No More Love on the Run)" goes gold.   Lionel Ritchie's *Can't Slow Down* wins Grammy.   Marvin Gaye shot and killed by his father.

1984 First MIDI sequencer, Roland MSQ700.   Emergence of personal computer in music production.

Armand Zildjian.

Paul Wennik.

In early 1984, Paul Wennik, New England Regional Director for Polygram Records, and Armand Zildjian, President and Chair of the Board of cymbal manufacturer Avedis Zildjian Company, were elected to the Board of Trustees.

Leonard Feather, President Lee Eliot Berk, and Oscar Peterson.

Honorary degree recipients at the 1984 Commencement exercises were author Leonard Feather and pianist Oscar Peterson. Jazz critic Feather, who died in 1994, edited *The Encyclopedia of Jazz*, one of the first scholarly books on the subject; he also produced records, composed songs, and played piano.

Joining jazz critic Martin Williams (center), before a history of jazz lecture, are (left to right) Voice Department faculty member Jan Shapiro, Voice Department Chair Kenneth Greenhouse, and faculty members Jeff Stout and Rob Rose.

Kenneth Greenhouse.

With the departure of Brian O'Connell, Kenneth Greenhouse was promoted to chair of the Voice Department in 1984. Since then, the department has almost doubled in size. Its innovative curriculum provides training in contemporary vocal styles including pop, Latin, country and western, and rhythm and blues, along with a solid foundation in traditional vocal techniques, and a special emphasis on vocal health. The lab program was revised to offer students the opportunity to concentrate on specific styles; labs in rehearsal techniques, advanced vocal performance, and small group performance were added. Many of the department's best students are regularly featured in the popular Singers' Showcase concerts.

John Scofield talks with students after a 1985 clinic.

Concerts and clinics in the first semester of the 1984-85 school year included a November performance by faculty member Jon Damian in a quartet with alumnus guitarist Bill Frisell. Another guitar alumnus, John Scofield, returned to conduct a clinic in February 1985.

Alumnus Bill Frisell (right) joins faculty member Jon Damian in concert at the Berklee Performance Center in November 1984.

Warrick Carter.

Dean Warrick Carter sits in with the Danish Radio Big Band.

For some years, many faculty members felt their contributions had been under-recognized. Some wanted more support for their professional growth and development. Others felt their voice insufficiently represented in the administration's decision-making process. In August 1984, Dr. Warrick Carter was hired as Berklee's first dean of faculty to help the college respond to these faculty concerns.

Dr. Carter came to Berklee from Governors State University in Illinois, where he was chair of the division of fine and performing arts. He was also a past president of the International Association of Jazz Educators and a former chair of the Music Advisory Panel, the National Endowment for the Arts. As a professional drummer, he performed and recorded with musicians such as Peabo Bryson and Natalie Cole.

Musicologist Eileen Southern (left) and Warrick Carter at a 1985 Black History Month panel discussion.

In 1992, the Office of the Dean of Faculty held an all-day retreat for division and department chairs.

Since 1984, the Office of the Dean of Faculty has worked on behalf of the faculty in many ways. Among the office's first actions was the development of criteria for faculty appointment, promotion, and retention, resulting in the establishment of the system of faculty rank common to most institutions of higher education. The Office of Faculty and Instructional Development, under the direction of Eric Kristensen, was established to provide faculty with support to improve their teaching skills and to obtain advanced degrees. Other faculty development programs were initiated, including substantial increases in travel support to attend professional conferences, a sabbatical leave program, and recording grants.

Faculty hiring has diversified in terms of race and ethnicity, and more women faculty members have been hired to reflect a changing educational and social environment. "That has had a real positive impact on minority and women students," says Dean Carter. "We are giving students role models in areas where they didn't exist before." In addition, more faculty with both academic and professional music credentials were hired from outside the Berklee community.

"The faculty are the college," Carter adds. "If we didn't have the quality of faculty we have, the college wouldn't have the name that it enjoys. It has been the faculty—the unsung heroes—that have done so much of the work."

Saxophonist Dave Liebman (playing piano) leads a 1987 faculty development workshop on improvisation instruction.

203

Dues Band founder Phil Wilson at the 20th anniversary concert.

A member of an early Dues Band, Richie Cole returned to help celebrate the group's 20th anniversary.

In December 1984, Phil Wilson celebrated the 20th anniversary of the Dues Band with a concert featuring special alumni guests saxophonist Richie Cole and trombonist Art Baron '68, and woodwind faculty member Bill Pierce, a former Dues Band member. Dues Band concerts were historically some of the most popular with students. When the Dues Band started performing in the late 1960s, "There would be this mob of students, hundreds of us, that would flood down Boylston Street to New England Life Hall for the concert," says Charles Chapman. "We'd tie up traffic, there were so many of us."

Inspired by Wilson's musicianship, sincerity, and good humor, the Dues Band played some of the most musically diverse programs heard at Berklee, ranging from classical to funk to jazz. Wilson continued to conduct ensembles but gave them different names, first the International Dues Band, and then the Rainbow Band, to reflect the increasingly international character of the Berklee student body.

1985 Chick Corea forms his Elektric Band.	John Carter records *Castles of Ghana*.	Pat Metheny and Ornette Coleman record *Song X*.	Miles Davis records 10-part suite *Aura*.
1985 Benefit concerts Live Aid and Farm Aid raise money for a variety of causes.	Whitney Houston hits the pop charts with her self-titled debut album. Madonna releases *Like a Virgin*.	Kate Bush releases *Hound of Love*.	VH-1 premieres.
		1985 Newly developed MIDI software for personal computers is used.	

During his March 1985 residency, Chick Corea rehearses a student band for a concert of his compositions.

Chick Corea conducts a master class in the synthesizer lab.

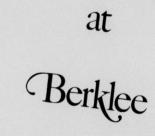

Chick Corea at Berklee

Corea conducting an advanced writing seminar.

In March 1985, keyboardist Chick Corea was in residence for a week at Berklee. The week's residency included master classes in the Advanced Synthesis Lab (which had opened in September 1984) and Music Production and Engineering studios (recently expanded at the beginning of the school year); master classes in piano and advanced writing; and general sessions for all the students. The highlight was a concert of new music composed and arranged by Corea for a Berklee student orchestra.

Anti-apartheid single "Sun City" released. Sade releases "Smooth Operator." REO Speedwagon's "Can't Fight This Feeling" goes gold. Foreigner releases "I Want to Know What Love Is." Tears for Fears album *Songs from the Big Chair* goes platinum.

Dean of Curriculum Gary Burton in his office . . .

. . . and on stage with a faculty all-star band featuring Bruce Gertz (center) and Greg Hopkins (right).

After hiring Dr. Carter as dean of faculty, questions of curricular leadership remained. Someone was needed to ensure that Berklee maintained its traditional strengths while guiding the curriculum as it evolved to meet the new demands of contemporary music. In March 1985, Gary Burton accepted the newly created position of dean of curriculum. "I feel Berklee gave me the tools that allowed me to adapt as music evolved and that's the most important thing," Burton says. "We have to give incoming students the tools that will serve them wherever they end up."

Since 1985, the Office of the Dean of Curriculum has managed the careful evolution of the roughly 800 courses Berklee offers. The office helped guide the evolution of the Music Synthesis and Songwriting majors and led in the creation of a distinctive educational identity for the Music Business/Management major first offered in 1992. Working with the Office of the Dean of Faculty, Burton and his staff also helped develop the cooperative master's degree program in jazz performance, writing, or pedagogy with the Boston Conservatory as well as the accelerated M.B.A. degree program with Suffolk University. With the promotion of David Mash to assistant dean of curriculum for academic technology in 1989, the office has also played a leading role in the incorporation of music technology into the Berklee curriculum.

"My years as dean have been fraught with irony," Burton says. "I'm an acoustic jazz musician who is a product of the old Berklee, yet I have overseen the transition of the school from being primarily a jazz school to being primarily a pop music school. I have overseen it going from a traditional teaching school to a technological world."

Associate Dean of Curriculum Robert Myers.

At the same time Gary Burton was appointed dean, Robert Myers was appointed associate dean of curriculum. Dr. Myers graduated from the Eastman School of Music and earned his doctorate at Northwestern University. The former chair of the music department at Saginaw Valley State College, Myers also had performed with musicians as diverse as country star Conway Twitty and free jazz saxophonist Ornette Coleman.

Dr. Myers has played a critical role in many important initiatives undertaken by the Office of the Dean of Curriculum. He supervised the course documentation process which developed a syllabus of every Berklee course and made them available to students. He also directed the course evaluation assessment procedure which created criteria for determining the effectiveness of courses based on educational outcomes. He coordinated campus-wide efforts to generate the Institutional Self-Study reports required for accreditation and has participated in the review committee which selects appropriate community and two-year colleges for articulation agreements. Articulation agreements allow students with the appropriate course work to transfer to Berklee after two years at participating colleges.

Larry Monroe performs with an all-star faculty ensemble at an outdoor concert at Boston's Museum of Fine Arts.

Larry Monroe instructs a class during the 1985 Berklee on the Road program in Barcelona, Spain.

An eventful spring of 1985 was capped by the implementation of a new divisional structure for the college administration. Each new division consisted of several departments with related concerns and was designed to help departments address common needs more effectively. "My father's modus operandi was mostly ad hoc—calling people together on an as-needed basis," explains President Lee Eliot Berk. "But as more and more people's opinions had to be consulted, it no longer was practical to work that way."

Larry Monroe '70 was appointed professional performance division chair, responsible for the Instrumental, Ensemble, Ear Training, and Performance Studies departments. Monroe joined the faculty in 1971 and taught instrumental and ensemble classes as well as ear training and theory. Among his other responsibilities, he supervised the recording of the "Jazz Beat from Berklee" radio series in the early 1980s.

As chair of the largest division at Berklee, Monroe has directed many initiatives with widespread impact. The Professional Performance Division has worked with the individual instrumental departments to strengthen proficiency exams and has worked to improve the instrumental lab program. The division has also directed efforts by the Ensemble and Performance Studies departments to reshape concert activities to more directly relate to the curriculum, resulting in more theme programs and departmental concerts. The division also coordinated a joint effort by several of the instrumental departments to create the Professional Performance Division MIDI Lab in 1989. It has evolved to meet the needs of students with differing levels of precollege training, adapted to a changing technological landscape, and changed to meet the increasing demand for rhythm instruments and decreasing demand for woodwinds and brass.

"The school's reputation and its willingness to make an instant adjustment to a block of students or musical trend is a big part of the early success of this school," Monroe says. "The jazz world was primarily defined by the wind players. Contemporary music, largely following rock music, is populated by rhythm instruments, guitar, piano, bass, and drums. It is a real trend in the world and we have to get in line with it."

Larry Monroe as a student at a
Recording Band rehearsal in 1970.

Ted Pease.

Don Puluse.

Other faculty members were also promoted to division chair positions. Ted Pease was selected to chair the Professional Writing Division, which includes the Commercial Arranging, Composition, Film Scoring, Jazz Composition, and (after 1986) Songwriting departments. Don Puluse was promoted to chair of the Music Technology Division, which incorporated the Music Production and Engineering and Electronic Music Department. The latter became Music Synthesis in 1986. After Puluse's promotion, Dave Moulton chaired the Music Production and Engineering Department. Associate Professor William Scheniman became chair in 1994.

**Associate Dean of Faculty
Ronald Bentley.**

**Associate Dean of Faculty Ronald Bentley with (left to right) President Lee Eliot
Berk and faculty members John Nelson and Richard Boulanger as they receive
Fullbright grant awards.**

At the same time division chair positions were created in 1985, Ronald Bentley was pro-moted to associate dean of faculty. Bentley joined the Guitar Department faculty in 1970, becoming assistant chair of the Guitar Department in 1975. From 1980 to 1985, he served as coordinator of instrumental studies and as an assistant to Adminstrator Robert Share.

In his new position, Bentley initially provided administrative continuity in the Office of the Dean of Faculty. His "insider's" perspective helped Dean Carter make the transition into his new position. Bentley manages important aspects of the day-to-day operations of the office. He administers the student evaluation process, academic payroll, and over-sees academic scheduling and facilities. In addition, he chairs the Institutional Academic Governance Committee, a broad-based group of representatives from throughout the Berklee community with the task of ensuring wide participation in decision-making on a range of academic and student policies.

Dean of Administration David Hornfischer.

Dean Hornfischer in the Berklee Bookstore with students Kevin Crosby (center) and Joes Canales who were awarded scholarships providing them with course-related text and matrerials.

David Hornfischer was promoted to dean of administration in the leadership reorganization of 1985. Hornfischer, who joined the Berklee staff in 1983 as director of administrative services, has an M.B.A. from the University of Massachusetts and is the former lead financial systems analyst at the Three College Computer Consortium, operated by Amherst, Mount Holyoke, and Hampshire colleges in central Massachusetts. Acting as the college's chief financial and administrative services officer, Hornfischer supervises the departments that provide the logistical support and infrastructure for Berklee's unique educational mission. These departments are Administrative Auxiliary Services, Comptroller, Human Resources, Information Systems, Payroll Services, Physical Facilities, and Publications.

Through effective fiscal planning under Dean Hornfischer's leadership and with continued strong demand for its unique programs, Berklee has been able to develop a solid financial base. When upgrading its financial rating of the college in 1993, Moody's Investors Service acknowledged Berklee's strong operating performance of the last decade as an important contributing factor, along with its substantial $60 million endowment and the broad base of its enrollment resulting from an international applicant pool.

Fredrick Miller, Assistant Dean of Administration
for Information Technology.

Leslie L. Montgomery, Assistant
Dean of Administration for Human
Resources.

Lois Goldstein, Assistant Dean of
Administration/Comptroller.

Staff members in the Office of the Dean of Administration work to strengthen and expand the college's human and financial resources. Dr. Leslie L. Montgomery was hired in 1987. She was responsible for creating a modern human resources department that meets the needs of Berklee's 500 faculty and staff and that includes their substaintial on-going input. Dr. Montgomery was promoted to assistant dean of administration for human resources in 1991 to reflect the growing magnitude of the human resource area and its positive impact on the Berklee community. Comptroller Lois Goldstein, who replaced retiring Comptroller Sam McNamee in 1990, administers the college's budgeting and bookkeeping for Berklee's $40 million of annual operations and has led the growth of the department to service many of the related financial needs of the college and its employees. Goldstein was promoted to assistant dean of administration in 1994. Since 1984, Judith Lucas has served as director of publications. During that period, the number and complexity of the college's design and publication needs intensified greatly with the increasing depth and richness of the college community itself and the increasing international recognition of Berklee throughout the world. Under her leadership, both internal and external publications successfully reflected the identity of a dynamic educational institution, with several receiving industry awards for excellence.

The Office of the Dean of Administration is also responsible for all new facilities and equipment. Some of the college's most critical new facilities are the responsibility of Assistant Dean of Administration for Information Technology Fredrick Miller, who offered critical information systems support in the installation of computers throughout the campus, and played a leading role in the creation of the Berklee Campus Local Electronic Fiber-based (B-CLEF) network. B-CLEF links Berklee's Boylston Street, Fenway, and Massachusetts Avenue buildings and facilitates electronic communication among faculty and staff. In addition, it will make possible the expanded use of music education technology and digital media throughout the campus in the proposed Berklee Learning Resources Network. Director of Physical Facilities Bruce Spena leads facility improvements and helps the department meet Berklee's maintenance needs.

Roy Haynes demonstrates his technique during a 1984 clinic.

Singer/songwriter Ricky Skaggs (left) with students.

Producer Roger Nichols (left) talks shop in a Berklee recording studio control room.

Performers and clinicians heard at Berklee during the 1984-85 academic year included jazz drummer Roy Haynes; singer/songwriter Ricky Skaggs; and Roger Nichols, producer of albums by Steely Dan and other bands.

Blues great B.B. King delayed a European tour to come to Berklee to accept an honorary degree in 1985.

Berklee honored its past and acknowledged its future with honorary degrees to Arif Mardin—one of its most distinguished alumni—and guitarist B.B. King—one of the greatest blues guitarists of all time and an important early influence on the development of rock music. For Mardin, it was an especially happy day as his son Joe became the second Mardin to receive a degree from Berklee College of Music.

215

Arif Mardin proudly holds his honorary degree at the 1985 Commencement.

Chapter Six

Berklee College of Music
1985 – 1995

In 1985, Berklee stood poised for change once again. In the next decade, the college embraced an ever-widening range of music styles and career opportunities. Education in popular music performance, songwriting, recording and production, and music business took on larger roles, while the traditional Berklee jazz performance and writing curriculum continued to be strong.

Berklee also became an educational leader in the field of music technology. The use of music synthesis and computer technologies as tools for composers and performers, and as a classroom enhancement for students and professors, grew steadily during the decade. By 1993, Associate Dean of Curriculum Robert Myers could write in the *Convocation Report* that "the notion of technology as a separate, invasive concept is disappearing."

In the United States, a severe economic recession coupled with a demographic decline and diminishing support for public school music programs took a toll on domestic enrollment. The college took several steps to help bolster enrollment. In Boston, Berklee expanded and refocused its community outreach and scholarship programs. The college expanded scholarship audition opportunities for U.S. students by starting national, multicity faculty tours. A Berklee Center in Los Angeles was opened and alumni chapters were formed.

International efforts included short-term study programs in Italy, Spain, Japan, Argentina, Brazil, and elsewhere. President Lee Eliot Berk conceived the Berklee International Network (BIN), a Berklee-led international consortium of schools of contemporary music that further strengthened interactions with international music educators, students, and alumni.

In its 50th year, Berklee, with alumni found in literally every area of the music industry, could celebrate a rich and varied history as one of the world's greatest contributors to the evolution of jazz and contemporary music.

1986 Tony Williams forms a new band with Wallace Roney and Bill Pierce.

Dexter Gordon stars in *Round Midnight*.

Sonny Rollins records *G-Man*.

1986 Paul Simon releases *Graceland*, giving exposure to African musicians.

The Rock and Roll Hall of Fame holds its first induction ceremony.

Janet Jackson releases her multihit album *Control*.

Peter Gabriel releases *So*.

Anita Baker releases "Sweet Love."

1986 PC-based digital audio (sample) editing possible.

Hard disk, digital-audio workstations (DAWs) commercially available.

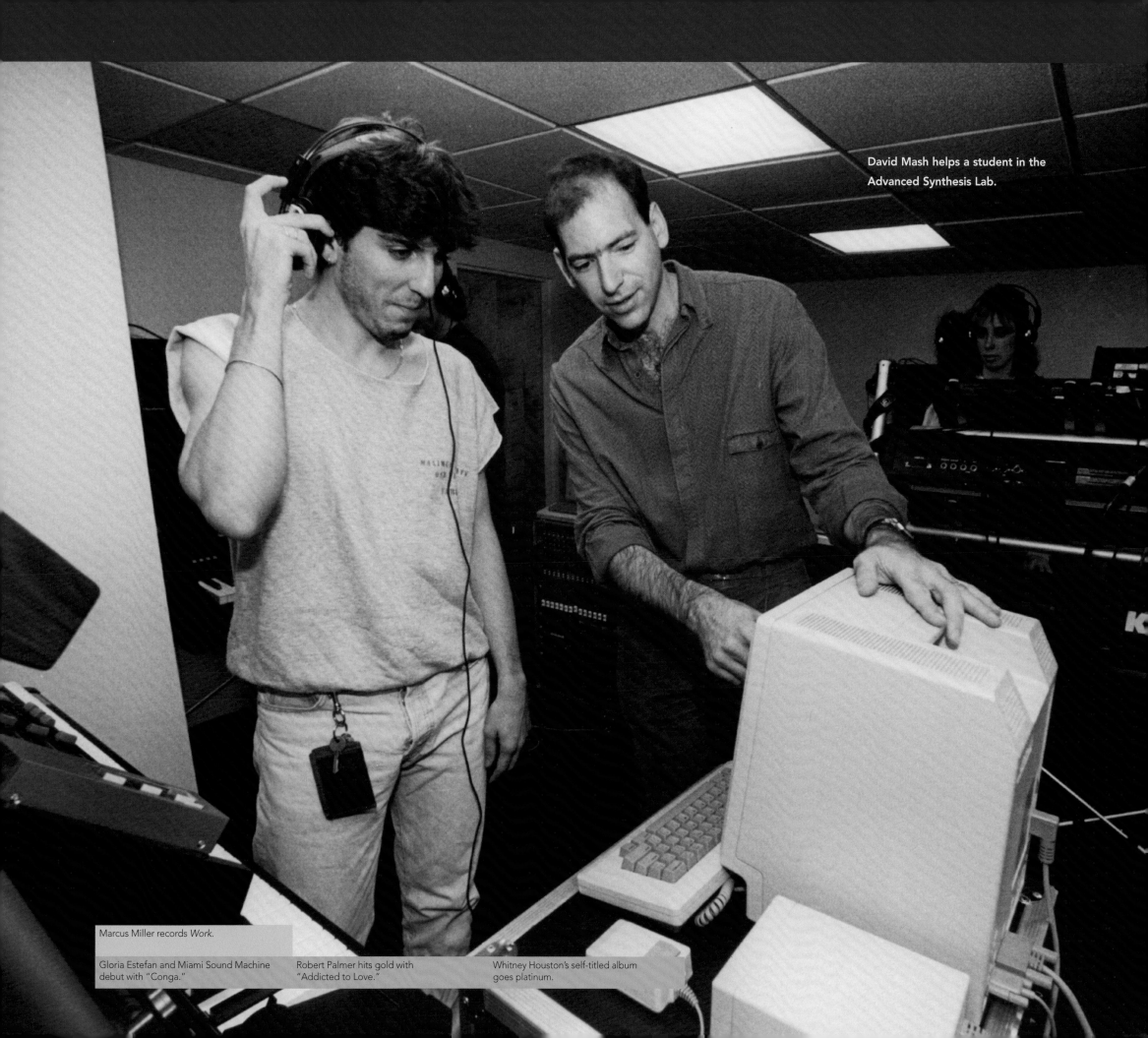

David Mash helps a student in the Advanced Synthesis Lab.

Marcus Miller records *Work*.

Gloria Estefan and Miami Sound Machine debut with "Conga."

Robert Palmer hits gold with "Addicted to Love."

Whitney Houston's self-titled album goes platinum.

Gary Burton performs at Berklee in Japan, one of the Berklee on the Road programs begun in 1985.

In July 1985, Berklee offered its first educational workshop abroad—Berklee in Japan. During the intensive week-long workshop, Berklee faculty members offered instruction in many aspects of effective jazz performance for students at all levels of ability. Berklee in Japan was the model for what grew into an enduring series of programs called Berklee on the Road.

The first of the Berklee on the Road series was offered in the fall of 1985 in Barcelona, Spain. In addition to several return visits to Japan and Spain, locations visited in the following years included: Heek, Germany; Rio de Janiero, Brazil; and Buenos Aires, Argentina. The annual two-week summer workshop at the Umbria Jazz Festival in Perugia, Italy, celebrated its 10th anniversary during Berklee's 50th anniversary year.

Larry Monroe and Gary Burton have coled the program since its inception. Drawing on his years of experience on the road as a professional musician, Monroe conceived the name for the program. Since its founding, the Berklee on the Road program has shared the Berklee approach to jazz education with students around the world, and assisted talented international students with Berklee scholarship support.

Larry Bethune conducts a clinic during the Berklee on the Road program in Barcelona, Spain.

Gary Burton directs a lesson via video monitor during a Berklee in Japan workshop.

The Berklee Reverence Gospel Ensemble with conductor Orville Wright and faculty member Dennis Montgomery III on piano.

Orville Wright.

At the beginning of the 1985-86 academic year, Orville Wright became chair of the Ensemble Department, supervising over 400 hours of playing activity per week at the college. A faculty member since 1974, Wright had taught arranging, harmony, ear training, and ensemble. He is a steel pan specialist and founder of Berklee's popular Reverence Gospel Choir. As chair of the Ensemble Department, he has helped revise criteria for the creation of new ensemble classes and ensured that Berklee students participating in departmental ensembles experience challenges typical of those found in music today.

Kenneth Pullig (third from left) performs with his jazz ensemble Decahedron at a 1979 concert.

At the start of the fall 1985 semester, Kenneth Pullig '74, a faculty member since 1975, became chair of the Jazz Composition Department. As a Berklee composition student, Pullig founded the jazz ensemble Decahedron for which he continued to compose and arrange as a faculty member. As chair of Jazz Composition, he developed jazz counterpoint courses, updated the senior portfolio project, and established the related senior portfolio recital series. He also established the departmental concerts, beginning in 1986 with "Fall, Together." "The Write of Spring" concert was established in 1992. In 1994, he chaired the space planning committee which evaluated ideas for the use of the new building at 921-925 Boylston Street, as well as the implications for improving effective use of existing facilities.

Kenneth Pullig.

Robert Freedman (right) and Father Norman O'Connor, a founding member of the Board of Trustees, at a WGBH broadcast by the Recording Band in 1958.

In the fall of 1985, Robert Freedman, a member of the faculty since 1983, was promoted to chair of the newly created Commercial Arranging major. The new Commercial Arranging major, offered for the first time during the 1985-86 academic year, was designed to prepare students to work as professional arrangers in a variety of styles and music industry settings. Besides offering courses in arranging for traditional instrumental ensembles and voice, the program has grown to include technology tools for the writer and MIDI applications.

222

Freedman had briefly taught at Berklee in the late 1950s, contributing arrangements to the first *Jazz in the Classroom* album before leaving to join Woody Herman in 1958. Freedman's varied background includes serving as musical director for Lena Horne, writing music for commercials, and composing music for films such as *One Trick Pony*, *The China Syndrome*, and *The Wiz*, for which he won a Grammy in 1978. In 1983, he was arranger for Wynton Marsalis' best-selling *Hot House Flowers* album. Freedman left the faculty in 1993 and was succeeded by Jay Kennedy in 1995. An award-winning composer, arranger, and producer of television commercial jingles, Kennedy has also written music for film, including *Wayne's World* and *The Electric Horseman*.

Robert Freedman performing with a faculty ensemble in 1987.

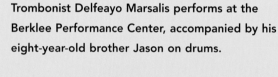

Trombonist Delfeayo Marsalis performs at the Berklee Performance Center, accompanied by his eight-year-old brother Jason on drums.

Branford and Wynton Marsalis.

A busy student performance schedule included a February 1986 concert by trombonist Delfeayo Marsalis '89, who led a group that included fellow students Julian Joseph '89 on piano and Javon Jackson '89 on tenor saxophone, plus special guests. Delfeayo later produced albums by brother Branford Marsalis and pianist Marcus Roberts, and performed with Elvin Jones. Pianist Joseph later recorded as a leader for the Atlantic label. Jackson later recorded and performed with Elvin Jones, Charlie Haden, and Art Blakey, and as a leader on the Blue Note label.

Delfeayo was not the only member of the acclaimed Marsalis family to attend Berklee. Earlier, older brother Branford Marsalis '80 attended Berklee before embarking on a career that included stints with Art Blakey, Sting, and as leader of the "Tonight Show" Orchestra.

223

Mike Scott, president of the Berklee chapter of the American Federation of Teachers/Massachusetts Federation of Teachers, and President Lee Eliot Berk sign the first contract between faculty and the administration.

In April 1986, faculty and administration signed their first collective bargaining agreement. The collective bargaining process began in April 1985 after faculty had voted to affiliate with the Massachusetts Federation of Teachers. At the time, most faculty felt that their conditions of employment, especially workload and pay, were not competitive with those of faculty at comparable colleges. The first contract was signed a year later, after a two-week faculty strike. Since then, the faculty and administration have signed two additional agreements, in 1989 and 1992, as the collective bargaining process has continued to address issues of comparable equity and other conditions of employment.

Faculty members vote to affiliate with the Massachusetts Federation of Teachers.

1987 Ornette Coleman records *In All Languages.*	Benny Carter releases *Central City Sketches.*	Wynton Marsalis releases *Standard Time,* volume 1.	James Newton records *Romance and Revolution.*	Michael Brecker releases *Michael Brecker.*
		1987 Michael Jackson's *Bad* is released, achieving more top 10 hits than any other album in pop history.		U2 releases *Joshua Tree.*
	1987 Breakthrough in hard-disk recording/editing within PC platform (ADAT and Sound Tools).		DAWs include Digidesign and R-DAT recorders.	

Herbie Hancock and Paul Simon during the 1986
Commencement ceremony.

Keyboardist Herbie Hancock and singer/songwriter Paul Simon received honorary
degrees at the 1986 Commencement. Hancock, whose career spans both jazz and popular music, joined the Miles Davis Quintet in 1964, and later scored pop music success in
1973 with "Chameleon" and in 1983 with the number-one hit single "Rockit." One of the
most skillful songwriters in popular music, Simon began his career in the late 1960s as
one-half of the Grammy Award-winning folk-rock duo Simon and Garfunkel. As a solo
artist, Simon won Grammys for his albums *Still Crazy After All These Years* and *Graceland*.

Ed Wilkerson and Eight Bold Souls release
self-titled debut.

Greg Osby and the Sound Theater recorded.

Terence Trent D'Arby makes U.S. debut.

The Beastie Boys go platinum with
Licensed to Ill.

Lisa Lisa and Cult Jam have gold single
with "Head to Toe."

Lawrence McClellan conducts a student seminar.

Lawrence McClellan, Jr.

Lawrence McClellan with a student in the Professional Education Division Technology Lab.

In August 1986, Lawrence McClellan, Jr., was hired as chair of the Professional Education Division, including the Music Education, Professional Music, and General Education departments. A former director of music education at the University of the Virgin Islands, Dr. McClellan received his Ph.D. from Michigan State University. As a performer he has appeared with Aretha Franklin, David "Fathead" Newman, and other jazz and pop artists.

Since McClellan's arrival, the division has grown significantly. In 1992, the Music Business/Management Department was established within the division. A Professional Education Division Technology Lab was created in 1993. And as the 50th anniversary year of 1995 approached, a search was concluded to appoint a founding chair for the college's newest department and major, Music Therapy. Dr. Suzanne B. Hanser, former chair of the Music Therapy Department at the University of the Pacific and a past president of the National Association for Music Therapy, joined the college in summer 1995 to organize course work and faculty for the initial offering of the new major in fall 1996. Since 1987, the division has been housed at 22 The Fenway, a former educational center for a religious order purchased and renovated by the college.

Jack Perricone during a Faculty Artist Series presentation.

Songwriting faculty member Pat Pattison addresses a group of
entering students.

Jack Perricone (right) awards singer/songwriter Bruce Cockburn with a
Distinguished Alumni Award.

In the fall of 1986, Berklee offered the first college-level major in Songwriting. Individual
songwriting courses, originally offered by faculty members Tony Teixeira and Jon Aldrich
in the early 1970s, had grown steadily in popularity. As a result, a committee was formed
to revamp existing courses and add subjects to the curriculum to form a new Songwriting
Department and major. After a national search, Associate Professor Jack Perricone was
promoted to chair of the new department in spring 1987.

Perricone, who holds a master's degree in composition from the University of Indiana,
had worked in the music publishing industry in New York and cowrote songs such as
the 1975 David Geddes hit "Run, Joey, Run" as well as songs for Angela Bofill and Lou
Rawls. As chair of the Songwriting Department, he developed the core curriculum for
the major, which incorporated faculty member Pat Pattison's innovative lyric writing
courses, and helped write the Business of Songwriting and Survey of Popular Song Styles
courses. He also helped plan and design the first MIDI Home Recording Studio, a college lab facility which opened in fall 1987.

"The program strikes a balance between academics and music-business reality," says
Perricone. "We emphasize craft, so in class we are not listening to a song in the same
way a producer would. We're working with technique, not judging a song for its commercial potential."

In 1985, David Mash directed La Mashine, a student synthesizer ensemble featuring Joe Mardin on drums.

David Mash in a Performance Synthesis class.

In 1986, the mission of the Berklee Electronic Music program was reconceived to take advantage of the rapid development of new technologies. Between 1978 and 1982, the use of synthesizers in live performance increased dramatically, thanks to the availability of polyphony (the ability to play more than one note at once), touch sensitivity, and programmable memory. Also in the early 1980s, digital sampling and the creation of a single standard for communications between electronic instruments, known as the Musical Instrument Digital Interface (MIDI), allowed musicians to connect computers and synthesizers, giving musicians access to a virtually unlimited universe of digitally stored sound, and unprecedented precision of control and editing.

To reflect these developments, the identity of the Berklee Electronic Music Department changed. It was renamed Music Synthesis and the curriculum was expanded and revised. Faculty member David Mash was selected to chair the new department while Electronic Music Department Chair Michael Rendish became assistant chair of the Film Scoring Department.

A Berklee alumnus, Mash joined the faculty full-time in 1976 and taught arranging, theory, and ensemble. He was a performing synthesist with trumpeter Donald Byrd, and in his own group Ictus. As a consultant he had worked with Kurzweil on implementing MIDI capability into their products, and with other hardware and software companies. Beginning in 1982, he offered the first Berklee courses in Performance Synthesis. In 1989, he was promoted to assistant dean of curriculum for academic technology and has conceived or administered the implementation of many of the most innovative educational applications of music technology at Berklee.

David Mash with students in the Advanced Synthesis Lab.

A Berklee education historically emphasized giving students the tools they needed for a career in music. As new tools were created, the curriculum expanded to accommodate them. At the Advanced Synthesis Lab, which opened at the beginning of 1986, students received hands-on instruction on the latest MIDI-equipped synthesis technology, drum machines, sequencers, and computers. MIDI and synthesizers were also introduced into the film scoring labs.

The computer's role in music education was growing also. In the fall of 1986, the Center for Computer-aided Instruction in Music, under the direction of William Brinkley '77, opened to give students and faculty alike the opportunity to learn and use these powerful tools. As efforts to familiarize faculty with new technology expanded and accelerated, the CCAIM gave way to a separate faculty facility, the Center for Technology in Music Instruction, under the direction of Tony Marvuglio. The Learning Assistance Lab, a separate facility where students could work on classroom assignments, was fully staffed and operational in 1988. A larger student facility, the Learning Center, opened in 1993.

Hal Chamberlain, David Mash, Dr. Raymond Kurzweil, Dr. Robert Moog, and President Berk at a 1987 Kurzweil demonstration.

231

Carla Bley perfoms with bassist Steve Swallow and guitarist Hiram Bullock as part of a major residency presentation at the Berklee Performance Center.

The major residency program was founded in 1986 with a week-long series of workshops and a concert by jazz composer Carla Bley and members of her orchestra. The residency offered more opportunity for interaction with the guest artist than could a single workshop. Members of Bley's orchestra, including Don Alias, Hiram Bullock, and former faculty member Steve Swallow, also conducted workshops while in residency. The concluding concert featured Bley's group with students and faculty playing her compositions and arrangements.

Carla Bley visits with Ken Pullig and Ted Pease during her major residency.

Carla Bley leads an ensemble including students and members of her band at the Berklee Performance Center.

Students perform in costumes from their native countries during International Folk Music Night concerts.

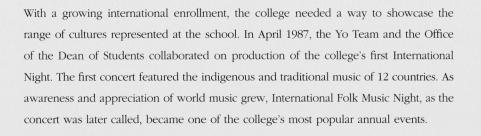

International Folk Music Night.

With a growing international enrollment, the college needed a way to showcase the range of cultures represented at the school. In April 1987, the Yo Team and the Office of the Dean of Students collaborated on production of the college's first International Night. The first concert featured the indigenous and traditional music of 12 countries. As awareness and appreciation of world music grew, International Folk Music Night, as the concert was later called, became one of the college's most popular annual events.

Art Blakey and Phil Ramone at the 1987
Commencement ceremony.

Two giants in very different fields of music—jazz drummer Art Blakey and pop record producer Phil Ramone—received honorary degrees at the 1987 Commencement ceremonies. Blakey led the Jazz Messengers for nearly 40 years, until his death in 1990, and frequently recruited Berklee alumni for his band, among them Keith Jarrett '63, Bill Pierce, Branford Marsalis, Donald Harrison, Geoff Keezer '89, and Delfeayo Marsalis. Seven-time Grammy Award-winner Ramone has produced major artists such as Billy Joel, Barbra Streisand, and Paul Simon, and composed motion picture soundtracks.

1988 Jackie McLean returns to recording with *Dynasty*.	Cecil Taylor records 10 CD boxed set of concert series in Berlin.	Latin jazz quintet Jerry Gonzalez and the Fort Apache Band record *Rhumba Para Monk*.	Clint Eastwood produces *Bird*, a film biography of Charlie Parker.
	1988 Singer/songwriter Tracy Chapman releases self-titled debut album.	Bruce Springsteen, Sting, Peter Gabriel, Tracy Chapman, and Youssou N'Dour tour world to benefit Amnesty International.	

Matt Betton receives his honorary doctorate from President Berk at the 1987 Entering Student Convocation.

Honorary doctorate recipient Dr. Raymond Kurzweil (center) with Dean Warrick Carter (left) and President Berk.

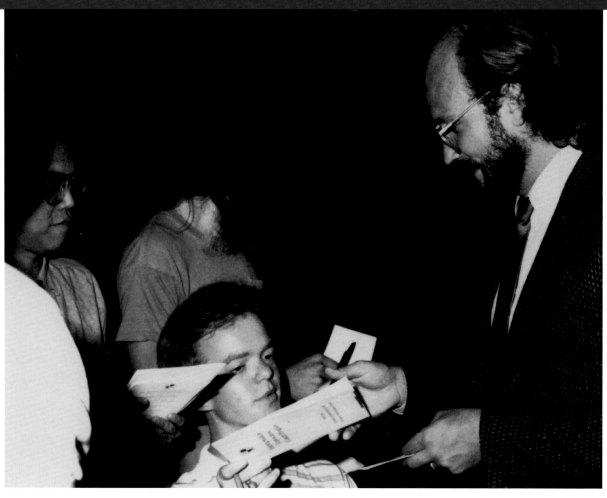

Alumni speaker John Scofield with students at the 1987 Entering Student Convocation.

The 1987-88 academic year started with Berklee's first Entering Student Convocation, an introduction to Berklee for the incoming class. The inaugural event featured remarks by college leaders, student and faculty representatives, and alumnus John Scofield. The college also conferred honorary degrees on synthesizer entrepreneur Raymond Kurzweil, founder of Kurzweil Music Systems, and Matt Betton, educator and founding executive director of the National Association of Jazz Educators (now called the International Association of Jazz Educators). The evening concluded with a concert produced by the Yo Team. "The idea is to make entering students feel like a class," says Dean of Students Lawrence Bethune, "and to introduce them to Berklee's history, philosophy, and educational mission." Since its establishment, Entering Student Convocation has served as an annual "rite of passage" for all new students.

Eric Clapton releases *Crossroads*, a 25-year anthology of his career.

Public Enemy releases *It Takes a Nation of Millions to Hold Us Back.*

George Michael wins Grammy for *Faith.*

Bobby McFerrin releases "Don't Worry, Be Happy."

Jazz guitarist Emily Remler performing at the 1988 Guitar Festival.

Mick Goodrick, Emily Remler, John Scofield, and John Abercrombie present a clinic . . .

In March 1988, an historic major residency underscored the impact of the Berklee Guitar Department on modern jazz guitar. A quartet of former William Leavitt students—John Abercrombie, Mick Goodrick, Emily Remler '76, and John Scofield—returned to Berklee for a series of clinics and workshops. For the first and only time in their careers, the four guitarists appeared together in concert at the Berklee Performance Center. Their appearance at Berklee was eloquent testimony to the school's pioneering role in guitar pedagogy. The gifted Remler recorded seven albums as a leader before she died of a heart attack in 1990, at the age of 32.

. . . and perform a concert during the 1988 Guitar Festival.

David Grusin with President Berk at the 1988
Commencement.

Dean Warrick Carter and Joe Williams.

Jazz singer Joe Williams, best known for his work with the Count Basie Orchestra, and
producer David Grusin, cofounder of GRP records with Larry Rosen, received honorary
degrees at the 1988 Commencement.

One Week
Performance
Program
August 7–11, 1988

Faculty members (left to right) Charles Chapman, Neil Olmstead, Jeff Stout, Dave Clark, and Ed Uribe at the first Berklee in Santa Fe program.

Gary Burton conducts a clinic during Berklee in Santa Fe.

In the summer of 1988, the college offered its first off-campus program within the United States, Berklee in Santa Fe (New Mexico), a week-long jazz performance program on the campus of St. John's College. The program provided an opportunity for greater numbers of students from the western United States to benefit from Berklee's unique approach to jazz education, just as students around the world had benefitted from similar Berklee on the Road programs overseas. It was repeated in 1989, after which off-campus programs for students in the western United States relocated to Los Angeles, California, where workshops have been presented annually thereafter.

Clark Terry performs with a student ensemble at the 1989 Entering Student Convocation concert.

Clark Terry with Armand Zildjian at the Entering Student Convocation.

The new academic year began with jazz trumpeter Clark Terry and Board of Trustees member Armand Zildjian, President and Chair of the Board of cymbal manufacturer Avedis Zildjian Company, receiving honorary doctorates at the 1989 Entering Student Convocation. Trumpeter Terry addressed the entering class and performed with a student ensemble.

Matt Marvuglio conducts a private lesson.

Jimmy Mosher, former chair of the Woodwind Department.

In September 1988, Matt Marvuglio '74 succeeded Jimmy Mosher as chair of the Woodwind Department. Marvuglio joined the Berklee faculty in 1974, teaching classes in theory, composition, and arranging. But his ability on a wide range of woodwinds, especially the flute, earned him a position with the Woodwind Department faculty. Well-versed on his many instruments, Marvuglio also mastered the new demands of the woodwind controller, becoming one of the best performers on the instrument at the college. His interest in music technology made him a major contributor to the development of the Professional Performance Division MIDI Lab.

Mosher, a former member of the Woody Herman and Buddy Rich big bands, joined the faculty in 1974 and had succeeded Joe Viola as chair in 1986. He died of cancer at the age of 49 in April 1987.

Trustee Alan Reese (seated, second from left) and the Financial Affairs Committee and consultants. Members of the committee include (standing, left to right): Trustee Richard Wilton, Dean David Hornfischer, Trustee James G. Zafris, Jr., Board of Trustees Chair William Davis, and President Lee Eliot Berk.

At the October 6, 1988, meeting of the Board of Trustees, William Falconer was elected trustee emeritus. Alan Reese, a partner in the international accounting firm of Coopers and Lybrand, was appointed to the Board of Trustees at the same meeting. Reese later chaired the board's Financial Affairs Committee, which has primary responsibility for the oversight of the college's operating and capital budgets, and management of the college's debt structure, endowment, and pension fund investments.

244

1989 Chick Corea releases *Akoustic Band.* Wynton Marsalis records *The Majesty of the Blues.*

1989 Rap and hip-hop added to MTV's format.

Roger Waters performs *The Wall* live at the Berlin Wall.

Living Colour's debut album *Vivid* peaks on charts.

Indigo Girls debut.

Milli Vanilli wins Grammy for Best New Group.

Berklee Jazz Ensemble pianist Julian Joseph at the keyboard.

The Berklee Jazz Ensemble (from left to right): Walter Beasley, Chris Cheek '91, Roy Hargrove, Tim Owens '89, Mashahiko Osaka '89, Paul La Duca '91, Delfeayo Marsalis, Antonio Hart, Julian Joseph, and Branford Marsalis.

Roy Hargrove performs during the Southern Comfort/IAJE Battle of the Collegiate Jazz Bands.

In January 1989, the Berklee Jazz Ensemble took first place honors in the ninth annual Southern Comfort/IAJE Battle of the Collegiate Jazz Bands. Supervised by faculty advisor Walter Beasley '84, the group included trumpeter Roy Hargrove. After leaving Berklee, Hargrove became one of the most frequently recorded jazz musicians of his generation. He attracted national attention with his own quintet, recorded with jazz legends such as saxophonists Joe Henderson and Johnny Griffin, and appeared as a sideman on dozens of albums. Alto saxophonist Hart later led his own groups and recorded for RCA.

Dave Holland records *Extensions*.   Don Pullen releases *New Beginnings*.   Marcus Roberts releases *Deep in the Shed*.

Paula Abdul's album *Forever Your Girl* goes platinum.   Fine Young Cannibals go platinum with *The Raw and the Cooked*.

Tom Plsek plays a didgeridoo, a traditional instrument of Australian aborigines.

Tom Plsek (right) with Slide Hampton at a 1987 visiting artist clinic.

Jazz trombonist J.J. Johnson (left) and Tom Plsek (far right) meet with students during a 1987 clinic.

In January 1989, the Trumpet Department and Trombone/Low Brass Department were consolidated into the Brass Department. Trumpet Department Chair Ray Kotwica was appointed distinguished chair, while Trombone/Low Brass Department Chair Tom Plsek became the chair of the new department. Plsek, after receiving his master's degree from the University of Houston, had joined the Berklee faculty in 1972. An organizer of and active performer in Sackbut Week, he is also a former president of the New England Computer Music Association and a performer and composer of contemporary music.

George Martin and Dizzy Gillespie at the 1989 Commencement.

Producer George Martin, best known for his work on landmark Beatles recordings such as *Help!* and *Sgt. Peppers' Lonely Hearts Club Band*, and jazz trumpeter Dizzy Gillespie, a major architect of bebop and Latin jazz, received honorary doctorates from Berklee at the 1989 Commencement ceremonies.

Ed Van Slyke, President Berk, and Don Puluse at the first
***Studio Production Projects* CD release reception.**

The June 1989 release of the CD *Studio Production Projects* marked Berklee's return to recording the best efforts of its students. The original purpose of the CDs was to show-case studio production projects of Music Production and Engineering students selected by a panel of faculty judges. Under the guidance of Dean of Curriculum Gary Burton, Berklee compact disc releases began to reflect the broader range of musical activity at the college. Singers' Showcase, the Vocal Jazz Ensemble, the Thelonious Monk Ensemble, the Reverence Gospel Choir, and, of course, Herb Pomeroy's Concert Jazz Orchestra, appeared on later releases.

This new series of recordings differed in significant ways from the *Jazz in the Classroom* series made by Pomeroy's Recording Band in the past. With state-of-the-art production facilities on campus and an academic major in Music Production and Engineering, record-ings were done at Berklee by students and faculty. The music recorded was no longer exclusively jazz either, but reflected the many contemporary music styles taught at Berklee.

John Lewis.

Milt Jackson.

Percy Heath.

Connie Kay.

The members of the Modern Jazz Quartet—pianist John Lewis, vibraphonist Milt Jackson, bassist Percy Heath, and drummer Connie Kay—received honorary doctorates at the Entering Student Convocation in 1989. Formed in 1952, the Modern Jazz Quartet played an enormously popular fusion of chamber music and cool bebop until Kay's death in 1994. Alumnus Gary Anderson, a former Woody Herman saxophonist who became a successful composer and producer, also addressed the entering students.

Jack Jarrett.

In July 1989, Composition Department Chair William Maloof retired after 27 years on the faculty. Jack Jarrett, former head of graduate studies in composition and conducting at Virginia Commonwealth University, was hired as the new department chair. Dr. Jarrett served as assistant conductor of the Richmond Symphony Orchestra and artistic director and conductor of the Richmond Opera Company. A composer of operatic, symphonic, and choral music, Jarrett is also the author of several software packages, including Music Printer Plus for IBM PC, Music Printer and Music Symbols for the Apple IIe, and MIDI Trigger. As department chair, Jarrett has continued to incorporate new technologies into the curriculum, introducing advanced courses in the conducting program and the use of MIDI technology to emulate the live orchestra experience in the conducting classroom.

| **1990** Gunther Schuller reconstructs and records Charles Mingus' "Epitaph." | Steve Coleman records *Rhythm People*. | John Zorn releases *Naked City*. | | |
| **1990** An AIDS benefit concert, "That's What Friends Are For," takes place. | Producers Jimmy Jam and Terry Lewis influence R&B and pop music. | Sinead O'Connor releases "Nothing Compares 2 U." | Janet Jackson's *Rhythm Nation* goes platinum. | M.C. Hammer releases *Please Hammer Don't Hurt 'Em*. |

Phil Wilson leads a student ensemble during the opening concert for the Lawrence and Alma Berk Recital Hall.

In October, a three-year effort to renovate performance facilities at the college culminated with the dedication of the new Lawrence and Alma Berk Recital Hall at 1140 Boylston Street. In his dedication remarks, Professional Performance Division Chair Larry Monroe noted, "Since this hall first opened to Berklee students in 1966, it has been full of music almost every day of the year," making it "one of the most active concert halls on the face of the planet." The refurbished auditorium features state-of-the-art audio and video equipment for both performance and classroom uses. Several faculty ensembles performed for the opening night festivities, including the Berklee All Stars, the Maggi Scott Quartet, the Phil Wilson-Paul Schmeling duo, the Larry Baione Trio, and the Greg Badolato Quartet.

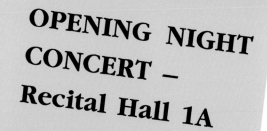

OPENING NIGHT CONCERT – Recital Hall 1A

Berklee
COLLEGE OF MUSIC

Monday, October 16, 1989
1140 Boylston Street, Recital Hall 1A
Boston, Massachusetts

Eddie Palmieri releases *Sueno*.	Charlie Haden and the Liberation Music Orchestra records *Dream Keeper*.	Wallace Roney records *Obsession*.	Marcus Roberts records *Alone with Three Giants*.
Neil Young and Crazy Horse release *Ragged Glory*.	Milli Vanilli's Grammy is revoked when it is revealed they did not sing on their album.	2 Live Crew spark censorship controversy with their album *As Nasty As They Wanna Be*.	En Vogue's "Hold One" goes platinum.	Mariah Carey's single "Vision of Love" goes gold.

Jerry Goldsmith and George Benson.

Academy Award-winning film composer Jerry Goldsmith and jazz-pop guitarist George Benson received honorary doctorates at the 1990 Commencement ceremonies.

Charles Combs (far left) leading a faculty panel (Judith Hanhisalo, Joe Coroniti, and Charles Cassara) at the first General Education symposium.

In July 1990, Dr. Charles Combs was appointed chair of the General Education Department. He earned his doctorate in theater and drama from the University of Wisconsin at Madison and came to Berklee from Plymouth State College in Plymouth, New Hampshire, where he was an associate professor and director of the college's rapidly growing theater program. As chair of the General Education Department, Combs directed the revision of department curriculum. As a result, greater emphasis was placed on courses in reading and writing skills and a wider variety of elective courses were made available.

Jack DeJohnette in performance during the Entering Student Convocation.

Voice of America producer and Berklee trustee Willis Conover, jazz drummer Jack DeJohnette, and high-school jazz educator William Stanley received honorary degrees at the 1990 Entering Student Convocation.

William Stanley, Jack DeJohnette, and Willis Conover.

On behalf of Japanese philanthropist/donor Mr. Genko Uchida, Junko Shishido (center), chief financial officer of the Uchida Scholarship Foundation, presents a $1 million donation to President Lee Eliot Berk during a ceremony in the Lawrence and Alma Berk Recital Hall. Also in attendance are (from left to right) Chancellor Lawrence Berk, Alma Berk, Uchida representatives Kensako Hogen and Shizuo Harada, and Trustee James Zafris, Jr.

UCHIDA SCHOLARSHIP FOUNDATION
101 LOMBARD ST., NO. 904-W
SAN FRANCISCO, CA 94111

№ 1297
11-40/107
1210

January 28 19 91

$ 1,000,000.00

Pay to the order of BERKLEE COLLEGE OF MUSIC

ONE MILLION DOLLARS

Sanwa Bank California
SAN JOSE OFFICE
BRANCH #107
220 ALMADEN BOULEVARD
SAN JOSE, CA 95113

Junko Shishido

Donation – Building Fund

In January 1991, the Uchida Scholarship Foundation presented the college with the largest single donation in the history of the college. In recognition of Berklee's unique contributions to international goodwill and understanding, the Japan-based foundation gave $1 million to the college to help it enlarge its educational facilities. In recognition of this extraordinary gift and his continuing support of Berklee programs in Japan, scholarships, and faculty-in-residence sponsorship, Mr. Genko Uchida was the first member elected to the newly created Board of Overseers in January 1992. After Berklee acquired important new property on Boylston Street in 1994, the college announced its intention of naming the building in honor of Mr. Uchida.

Pat Metheny performs with Gary Burton and a
student ensemble during his major residency.

Janis Ian at a songwriting clinic in April 1991.

Gunther Schuller at a clinic in March 1991.

In April 1991, former faculty member Pat Metheny took part in a major residency, during which he and Dean of Curriculum Gary Burton performed with a student quartet.

Visiting artists in 1990-91 included Pulitzer Prize-winning composer Gunther Schuller,
author of several books of jazz history and analysis, and Janis Ian, best known for the
hit songs "Society's Child" (which she wrote and performed at the age of 14) and "At
Seventeen."

Phil Collins joins students on stage during the 1991 Commencement concert.

Rock superstar Phil Collins, Cochair of the Board and Cochief Executive Officer of Atlantic Records Ahmet M. Ertegun, and jazz singer Al Jarreau each received honorary doctorates at the 1991 Commencement. During the musical tribute to him at the Commencement concert, Collins thrilled both the audience and student performers by making an unscheduled appearance on stage.

Al Jarreau, Ahmet Ertegun, and Phil Collins.

Roy Haynes, Joe Zawinul, President Berk, and
Ikutaro Kakehashi at the 1991 Entering Student
Convocation.

At the 1991 Entering Student Convocation, alumnus Joe Zawinul, best known as keyboardist and primary composer with jazz-rock fusion group Weather Report, received an
honorary doctorate, along with veteran jazz drummer Roy Haynes, and Roland
Corporation Chief Executive Officer Ikutaro Kakehashi. Mr. Kakehashi established a
Roland Scholarship Fund at Berklee in 1990. Drummer Terri Lyne Carrington was the
alumni speaker.

1991	Miles Davis dies.	Wynton Marsalis appointed artistic director of the new Jazz at Lincoln Center program.
1991 Seattle "grunge" band Nirvana releases "Smells Like Teen Spirit."	R.E.M. releases "Losing My Religion."	L.L. Cool J. releases "Mama Said Knock You Out."	Metallica releases *Metallica*.

Steven Lipman (far right) address a group of Berklee alumni representatives.

Alegria Montero.

At the beginning of the fall 1991 semester, Director of Admissions Steven Lipman '69 and Director of the Counseling Center Alegria Montero, each received promotions to assistant dean positions. Lipman joined the Berklee staff in 1970 and worked as head of tutoring services and as an assistant to Dean Gerald Siddons. In 1974, he became director of admissions and led the development of the office from a mostly domestic student admissions department to an international one, encompassing global marketing, recruitment, and admissions operations. Emily Woolf Economou succeeded Lipman as director of admissions in 1994. Economou, who joined the Admissions Office staff in 1985, holds a master's degree in higher education administration from Boston College.

Dr. Alegria Montero joined the Berklee staff in 1984 as director of counseling, replacing founding director Jeff Callahan. Montero holds a doctorate in higher education administration from the University of Massachusetts and served as a senior counselor and placement coordinator at North Shore Community College before coming to Berklee. As assistant dean, Montero has upheld a high standard of service and advocacy for students and met the increasingly diverse needs of an international student population. Assistant Director of Counseling Jill Ritchie was promoted to director of counseling.

| Branford Marsalis records *The Beautyful Ones Are Not Yet Born.* | Anthony Braxton records 4-CD set *Willisau 1991.* | Terence Blanchard releases *Simply Stated.* | Sonny Sharrock records *Ask the Ages.* | |
| Tony, Toni, Toné, the Brand New Heavies, and Mint Condition update classic R&B sound. | Garth Brooks releases *Ropin' the Wind.* | Guns N' Roses release *Use Your Illusion I and II.* | C & C Music Factory earns platinum sales with *Gonna Make You Sweat.* | Luther Vandross wins Grammy for "Power of Love/Love Power." |

Danny Gatton . . .

. . . and John Abercrombie perform at the William Leavitt Memorial Concert.

In November 1991, a memorial concert for Guitar Department Chair William Leavitt, who had died in November 1990, paid tribute to a beloved member of the Berklee faculty and a man many consider the most important individual in contemporary guitar education. Summarizing Leavitt's contributions to guitar education in the concert program, Larry Monroe wrote that before William Leavitt started teaching at Berklee "there was no established pedagogy, no repertoire, no books of etudes, and no scholarship to address the musical and educational needs of aspiring student guitarists. . . . Under Bill Leavitt's leadership, these challenges were met and overcome with the development of innovative methods . . . which became study standards throughout the world."

Former Leavitt students John Abercrombie and Mick Goodrick opened the concert in a quartet featuring bassist John Lockwood '77 and former faculty member Gary Chaffee on drums. Larry Baione '71, Leavitt's successor as chair of the Guitar Department, played a solo in tribute to his late mentor and colleague. Headliner Danny Gatton closed the evening with a set of his rousing blend of instrumental rhythm and blues, bebop, country, and rockabilly.

Larry Baione (right) gives a
private lesson.

Larry Baione joined the guitar faculty in 1977 and served as assistant chair to William
Leavitt from 1987. After Leavitt's untimely death in 1990, Baione was appointed chair. As
chair of the largest instrumental department at Berklee, Baione has overseen the expansion and revision of guitar labs to include a wider number of styles and techniques as
well as labs in guitar synthesizer and electronic effects.

Billy Joel.

Ben Riley rehearsing with a faculty ensemble for a Berklee Performance Center concert.

Max Roach.

A clinic on songwriting and the music business by singer/songwriter Billy Joel was a highlight of the presentations by visiting artists during the 1991-92 academic year. In February, jazz drummer Ben Riley, best known as Thelonious Monk's drummer from 1964 to 1967, conducted a major residency that culminated in a Performance Center concert with a student ensemble. In May, legendary jazz drummer Max Roach also conducted a clinic.

James G. Zafris, Jr., President Lee Eliot Berk, and William Davis.

At the January 1992 Board of Trustees meeting, James G. Zafris, Jr., stepped down as chair after serving in that capacity since November 1970. Berklee had undergone years of steady growth while Zafris chaired the board. In acknowledgement of his contributions to Berklee's growth and ongoing commitment to educational excellence, the board established the James G. Zafris, Jr., Distinguished Lecture Series. The series endowed an annual lecture by a music-industry speaker on a topic of relevance to those enrolled in the new Music Business/Management major. Zafris remains on the board as chair of the Institutional Advancement Committee.

William Davis was elected to succeed him at the January meeting. A member of the board since 1977, Davis is a senior vice president at Donaldson, Lufkin, and Jenrette, an international investment firm.

Bonnie Raitt receives applause from the audience at the 1992
Commencement concert.

Grammy Award-winning singer/songwriter Bonnie Raitt and Joe Smith, President and
CEO of Capitol-EMI Music, received honorary degrees at the 1992 Commencement.

Professional Performance Division Chair Larry Monroe,
Bonnie Raitt, President Berk, and Joe Smith.

At the 1992 Entering Student Convocation, BMI President and CEO Frances W. Preston and drummer Peter Erskine received honorary degrees. *Esquire* magazine once singled out Preston as "the most influential and powerful person in the country music business." She became president and CEO of BMI in 1986. Drummer Erskine is best known for his work with Weather Report and Steps Ahead.

Frances Preston and Peter Erskine
with President Berk.

Student Melvin Butler '93 solos during the Entering Student Convocation concert.

Don Gorder.

Don Gorder (left) with Tom Sturges, President of Chrysalis Music Group (second from left), and Music Business/Management faculty member Schuyler Traughber (rear) in the Professional Education Division Technology Lab. Sturges was the 1994 Zafris Distinguished Lecture Series speaker.

A new major in Music Business/Management was offered for the first time in the 1992-93 academic year. Individual courses in business-related topics had been offered at Berklee since the late 1960s, when President Lee Eliot Berk offered the first course in music law. But the new major took a more comprehensive approach, with courses designed to help students develop a variety of business skills.

Donald Gorder was hired as chair of the new department in 1991. Gorder brought experience in music, law, academia, and business to his position. He chaired music business programs at two other universities prior to coming to Berklee. He received a law degree from the University of Denver and worked as an entertainment lawyer specializing in contracts and copyright issues. A professional trumpeter, he also holds a master's degree in jazz pedagogy from the University of Miami.

As chair of the new department, Gorder oversaw the creation and implementation of an innovative course of study. In addition to general business topics, new courses covered international industry operations in record and music publishing companies, concert promotion, and the roles and functions of agents, managers, and attorneys. For students who wanted an advanced degree, a joint accelerated M.B.A. program with Suffolk University was instituted.

1992 Alternative rock bands such as Primus and Alice in Chains enter charts.   Rapper Ice T's *Cop Killer* sparks controversy.   Rock the Vote encourages young people to vote in the presidential election.   Country singer Wynonna Judd releases self-titled solo debut album.

President Lee Eliot Berk (second from left) with representatives from the Centre of Music Studies Phillipos Nakas (left to right) Leonidas Arniakos, Konstantinos Nakas, and Despina Nakas after signing on as part of the Berklee International Network.

Professional Performance Division Chair Larry Monroe (left) and President Berk (right) with Spain's L'Aula de Musica President Arthur Bernstein.

In 1992, Berklee established its first formal relationships with music schools in other countries. For many years, the college had received requests from talented alumni and others who wanted authorization to set up Berklee-affiliated schools in their home countries. In addition, established schools wanted to create formal links with the college. President Lee Eliot Berk evolved the concept of the Berklee International Network (BIN) as a way of helping emerging schools of contemporary music improve educationally while providing students with greater international access to Berklee. The charter members of BIN were the L'Aula de Musica in Barcelona, Spain; the Rimon School of Jazz in Tel Aviv, Israel; and the Phillipos Nakas Centre of Music in Athens, Greece. In October 1994 the Pop Jazz Conservatory in Helsinki, Finland, and the American School of Modern Music in Paris, France, joined the growing network.

Berklee faculty and staff visit each network school to discuss educational, technological, and administrative issues. Each school serves as a center at which students and area aspiring musicians can audition for Berklee scholarships. BIN schools often become stepping stones for international students to attend Berklee. The college has benefited from the opportunity to learn more about the culture, accomplishments, and needs of international music education and has welcomed many of the leaders, faculty, and students from BIN schools to the campus. A steering committee, chaired by Professional Performance Division Chair Larry Monroe, was established to manage the network, plan for expansion, evaluate schools that apply for membership, and schedule visits and exchanges. Assistant to the President for Education and Community Partnerships J. Curtis Warner, Jr., plays a key role in maintaining coherence in all network activities.

President Lee Eliot Berk and Mrs. Susan G. Berk (center) celebrate the founding of the Berklee International Network with (from left) Amikam Kimelman, Israel's Rimon School President Orlee Sela, and (right) Harry Lifshitz, and Yehuda Eder.

Curtis Warner leads a theory class with a former student coordinator of the college's mentoring program Angie Payne '94 (seated) and Boston Latin Academy student Mark Goncalves.

Curtis Warner (right) presents an award to Roland Hayes Division of Music representative Robert Winfrey for their outstanding contribution to secondary education.

In 1992, J. Curtis Warner, Jr. '76 joined the staff as assistant to the president for education and community partnerships to coordinate the college's many community service programs and to administer the Berklee International Network. Warner had previously taught in the Boston schools, becoming assistant head master at Dorchester High in 1986.

1992 Joe Henderson releases *Lush Life.*   Mario Bauza releases *Tanga Suite.*   Geri Allen releases *Maroons.*   Don Byron releases *Tuskegee Experiments.*

Bruce Springsteen releases *Human Touch* and *Lucky Town.*   Billy Ray Cyrus releases *Some Gave All.*   Eric Clapton releases "Tears in Heaven."   TLC releases platinum single "Ain't 2 Proud 2 Beg."

SYSTEM 5 scholarship winners are showcased at the end of each summer's program in a concert presented for the local community.

Boston Mayor Ray Flynn presenting President Berk with the first Institutional Award of Exemplary Public Service.

Mentoring coordinator Adrian Ross '96 performs with his jazz ensemble at the Berklee Performance Center.

Berklee already had a long history of service to the Boston community. Community service efforts were first formalized in 1971 with the Community Service Program and continued to grow as President Lee Eliot Berk established the Office of Community Affairs. In 1990, the city of Boston recognized Berklee's many contributions with its first Institutional Award of Exemplary Public Service.

Executive Assistant to the President Tom Riley '78 put the weight of the President's Office behind expanded community outreach that emphasized equipment donations to Boston public schools, training support to Boston public school music teachers, and scholarship support to Boston public school students. Riley had joined the Berklee staff in 1986 as assistant to the president and was promoted to executive assistant in 1992 as his role expanded.

The foundation for many of Berklee's community service efforts is the Berklee City Music program, which offers at-risk Boston high school students college-level music education through one-on-one mentoring sessions and scholarship opportunities. Berklee faculty and upper-level students in the Public Service through Music Club provide private lessons, theory classes, and ensemble coaching for Boston-area students so that they can prepare for college music studies.

Scholarships to Berklee's Five-week Summer Performance Program are awarded through the Summer Youth Scholarship for Talent and Excellence in Music program (SYSTEM 5). Each summer, a number of SYSTEM 5 participants receive scholarships for full-time study at Berklee.

269

Brass Department Chair Tom Plsek, Jazz Composition Department Chair Ken Pullig, and Ear Training Department Chair Greg Badolato performing in concert.

Chair of the Ear Training Department Steve Plummer retired in 1992. A classically trained pianist who graduated from Boston University, Plummer began teaching at Berklee in 1964, becoming chair of Ear Training in 1982. As chair, Plummer helped revise the Ear Training curriculum, directed the development of tutorial services, and contributed to the establishment of criteria for measuring musical, educational, and teaching effectiveness.

Plummer was succeeded by Greg Badolato. Badolato joined the Berklee faculty in 1982, teaching woodwinds, theory, and ensemble. A professional woodwind player of wide experience, Badolato has performed with the Belgium Philharmonic Orchestra, singer Sammy Davis, Jr., jazz drummer Art Taylor, and many others. As assistant chair of the Ear Training Department, he was a major contributor to the revision of the curriculum and was instrumental in training faculty in the department's new program.

Greg Badolato.

| **1993** Joe Henderson releases *So Near, So Far.* | Henry Threadgill and Very, Very Circus release *Too Much Sugar for a Dime.* | Dizzy Gillespie dies. | Cassandra Wilson releases *Blue Light 'Til Dawn.* |
| **1993** Eric Clapton records in an acoustic "unplugged" format. | Boys II Men and Sisters With Voices (SWV) revive popularity of vocal harmony groups. | Pearl Jam releases *Ten.* | |

Barbara London, Chair of the Harmony Department.

Alex Ulanowsky.

In March 1993, Associate Professor Alex Ulanowsky '70 died unexpectedly in his home at the age of 50. He began teaching at Berklee in 1971 and in 1973 was named chair of the Harmony Department, a position he held until 1981, when he became chair of the Core Studies Department. In 1983, he left the administrative position to return full-time to teaching. A pianist, he had toured with the Buddy Rich Band in 1973 and with jazz singer Jon Hendricks in 1982, and performed with countless student and faculty ensembles throughout his 22 years of teaching at Berklee.

Barry Nettles '68, who joined the faculty in 1972, succeeded Ulanowsky as chair of the Harmony Department, serving from 1985 to 1993. Assistant Professor Barbara London was promoted to chair of the Harmony Department in 1993, becoming Berklee's first woman department chair. A jazz flutist who has led her own groups and performed with bassist Richard Davis, trumpeter Clark Terry, and others, London joined the Berklee faculty in 1986.

271

Frank Zappa dies. Liz Phair releases *Exile in Guyville*. PJ Harvey releases *4-Track Demos*.

1993 CD-ROM commercially available.

Dean of Institutional Advancement John Collins.

President Lee Eliot Berk and Mrs. Susan G. Berk (center) with students at the first Annual Fund Phonathon.

In April 1993, John Collins was promoted to dean of institutional advancement. Collins, who joined the Berklee staff in 1989 as director of development, had previously worked in alumni relations at Tufts University and Emerson College. His promotion reflected an increased long-range emphasis on external relations as the college sought more resources for scholarship and educational programs.

Under his leadership, alumni and media outreach grew. The establishment of alumni chapters in major music industry centers and publication of *Berklee today*, the college's alumni magazine, improved and strengthened alumni relations. Support from all donor constituencies grew substantially. In 1993, Rob Hayes joined the staff as director of public information, and continued to maintain Berklee's high profile in the media. Alma Berk retired as chief public affairs officer in August 1994.

"Alumni are a measure of an institution's success and Berklee alumni are our best advertisement around the world," says Collins. "As our alumni body makes an ever greater impact in the music industry, corporations will increasingly recognize that investing in Berklee is an investment in the future of music."

The first annual Encore Night saluted conductor and Berklee
Trustee Harry Ellis Dickson on his 85th birthday.

Johnny Mandel, President Berk, Dean of Faculty Warrick Carter, and Billy Joel.

Pop star Billy Joel and composer and arranger Johnny Mandel, whose compositions include "The Shadow of Your Smile" and "Suicide Is Painless" (the theme to *M.A.S.H.*) received honorary degrees at the 1993 Commencement.

Commencement speaker Joel said to the graduating class, "If you make music for the human needs you have within yourself, then you do it for all humans who need the same things. Ultimately, you enrich humanity with the profound expression of these feelings."

Patricia Doyle is welcomed by President Berk to the Board of Trustees.

David Lee and President Berk at the June 1993 meeting of the Board of Trustees.

At its June 1993 meeting, the Board of Trustees elected two new members: Patricia A. Doyle, a financial advisor with Institutional Credit Enhancement, a company that provides financial services to colleges, high schools, and other nonprofit institutions; and David Lee, Vice President of Stull and Lee, a leading Boston architectural and urban design firm. Doyle serves on the board's Financial Affairs Committee. Lee is a member of the board's Institutional Advancement Committee.

Joe Smith.

Students perform at the annual Professional Writing Division concert.

Faculty member Garrison Fewell performs at a Professional Writing Division concert.

In July 1993, Joseph Smith '75, was appointed chair of the Professional Writing Division, succeeding Ted Pease, who was appointed Berklee's first distinguished professor when he returned to full-time teaching. Smith had scored many television programs and films, including "Star Trek: The Next Generation," *Bull Durham*, and *Missing in Action III.* He also had arranged for Ben Vereen, Yellowjackets bassist Jimmy Haslip, Kenny Loggins, and many others. "I believe my strength, in having come from working in the industry is in directing the writing and core curriculum to meet the everyday demands of today's professional musician," Smith says. "This process involves retaining traditional music education and combining that with the teaching of modern industry technology."

Lester Menezes '94, winner of the John Dankworth Award, performs at the 1994 Professional Writing Division Concert.

The 40-station Learning Center.

Years of increasing use of educational technology at Berklee culminated in the opening of the Learning Center, the world's largest and most sophisticated networked computer learning facility for music education, in September 1993. The center makes more technology available to more students than ever before in Berklee's history, providing them with unprecedented resources. "The establishment of the facility was a revolutionary step. It basically gives every Berklee student access to technology," says Assistant Dean of Curriculum for Academic Technology David Mash, who played a critical role in creating the center.

The center, which is under the direction of Michael Badolato, houses 40 computer-synthesizer workstations, four independent tutoring rooms equipped with workstations, and 15 tape deck stations. Each workstation is outfitted with a computer with CD-ROM drive, 14" color monitor, synthesizer, MIDI interface, mixer/cassette deck, and head-

phones. Connected to a local area network, the workstations support file sharing, print spooling, and bulletin board activities. Students can access self-paced tutorials and other instructional software that reinforces class work; productivity tools such as music sequencing, notation, and word processing; and a library of retrievable audio and video resources. After the Learning Center opened, all entering Berklee students were required to take an Introduction to Music Technology course.

The Learning Center replaced the Learning Assistance Lab at 22 The Fenway, which was converted to the Professional Education Division Technology Lab. The lab provides technology training for students majoring in Music Education, Professional Music, and Music Business/Management.

1994 Whitney Houston wins Grammys for the soundtrack to *The Bodyguard.*   Country and R&B stars collaborate on *Rhythm and Country and Blues.*

Alan Paul, Cheryl Bentyne, President Berk, Michael Greene, Janis Siegel, and Tim Hauser at the 1993 Entering Student Convocation.

At the 1993 Convocation, Tim Hauser, Janis Siegel, Alan Paul, and Cheryl Bentyne, members of the Grammy-winning vocal quartet Manhattan Transfer best known for their vocalese version of Joe Zawinul's "Birdland," received honorary degrees. Industry speaker, Michael Greene, President and CEO of the National Academy of Recording Arts and Sciences, also received an honorary degree.

Manhattan Transfer perform at a clinic before receiving their honorary doctorates.

1994 Wynton Marsalis releases *In This House, On This Morning.*   Joshua Redman releases *Mood Swing.*

Kurt Cobain, lead vocalist of Nirvana, commits suicide.   Paul McCartney, George Harrison, and Ringo Starr collaborate on a recording to celebrate the 30th anniversary of the formation of the Beatles.   Hole releases *Live Through This.*   Stone Temple Pilots release *Purple.*

1994 PC-based multimedia production begins.

Alumnus Jan Hammer at a film
scoring clinic.

Will Calhoun presenting a drumming clinic.

Afro-pop singer Salif Keita (left) and Executive
Assistant to the President Tom Riley.

Visiting artists included two prominent alumni. Will Calhoun, drummer for the rock band
Living Colour, visited in November. Jan Hammer, keyboardist with the jazz fusion group
Mahavishnu Orchestra and a Grammy winner for his theme to the "Miami Vice" televi-
sion program, discussed his latest movie soundtrack at his lecture. Afro-pop vocalist Salif
Keita was also a visiting artist.

Gene Joly.

Sandra Uyterhoeven.

In January, two new members joined the Board of Trustees. Sandra Uyterhoeven, Assistant Director of Management Systems for the Massachusetts Water Resources Authority and a treasurer of the Board of Directors of the Boston Harbor Association, was elected to the board in January 1994. At the same meeting Gene Joly '73, president of E.U. Wurlitzer Music and Sound and a member of the Board of Directors of the National Association of Music Merchandisers, was also welcomed to the board.

Peter Gordon and Alan Silvestri at
the first Taking Care of Business alumni
seminar in Los Angeles.

Reflecting a new commitment to strengthening relationships between the college, Los
Angeles-area alumni, and the music industry, the Berklee Center in Los Angeles opened
in the spring of 1993. Under the direction of Peter Gordon '78, the busy office works to
increase access to information about Berklee for talented area music students, cultivates
potential relationships with corporations, and plans alumni club networking, career
advancement, and continuing education events. In October 1994, the first in a series of
alumni seminars, entitled Taking Care of Business, featured guest speaker film composer Alan Silvestri '70, whose screen credits include *Forrest Gump*, *Who Framed Roger
Rabbit?*, and all three *Back to the Future* films. Gordon, a former Berklee faculty member and an active studio saxophonist, say the center provides "an opportunity to help
Berklee become regarded as the higher education center of the music industry."

Jazz and pop singer Nancy Wilson and English rock star Sting received honorary degrees at the 1994 Commencement. Sting delivered a stirring Commencement address in which he said, "Music puts me in touch with something beyond the intellect, something other-worldly, something sacred."

Jonathan Royal '95 takes center stage at the 1994 Commencement concert.

Sting and Nancy Wilson at a press conference after the 1994 Commencement.

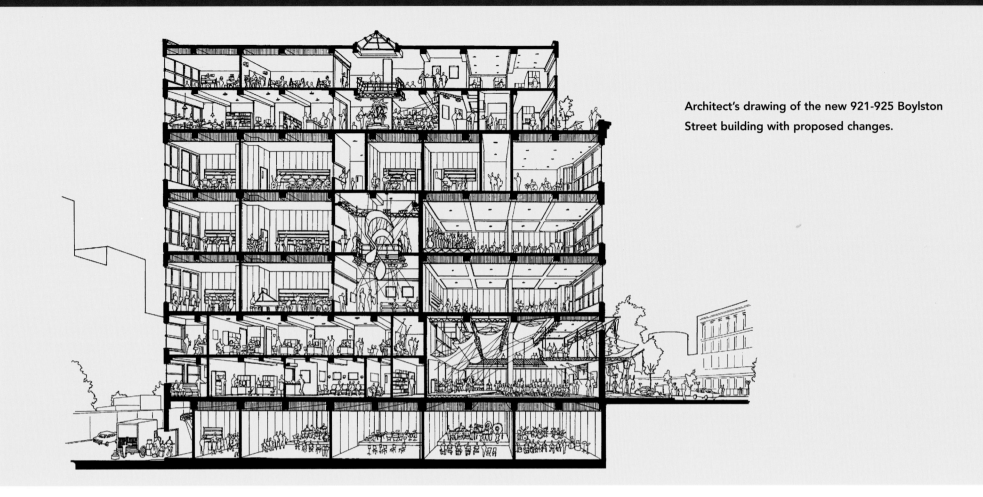

Architect's drawing of the new 921-925 Boylston Street building with proposed changes.

After seven years of growth since opening its last major property acquisition, 22 The Fenway, Berklee was once against feeling cramped for space. An explosion in course offerings, including a new major in music therapy, created demand for more classrooms. New rehearsal space and private practice rooms were needed to accommodate a new ensemble workshop program and growing numbers of guitar and percussion students. But as the college devoted more and more of its existing facilities to computer-based laboratories, the space available for these traditional uses grew more limited. In June 1994, the college acquired two new buildings located at 921-925 Boylston Street to help alleviate its space crunch. The additional 40,000 square feet increased educational and administrative facilities by roughly 16 percent.

After several months of planning and discussion, a master plan was submitted to the Board of Trustees. Two college committees working with planning specialists Miller Dyer Spears, developed the plan. A Space Planning Steering Committee consisting of President Lee Eliot Berk, college deans, and trustee David Lee was responsible for the overall direction of the planning process. Ken Pullig chaired the 25-member committee that came up with specific recommendations for use of the new property and existing facilities.

The proposal submitted in February 1995 called for consolidating student affairs offices, creating a medium-sized 200-seat performance space, and relocating the Percussion and Guitar departments to larger facilities at the Boylston Street properties. Recommendations for other Berklee facilities included an enlarged library and Film Scoring Department at 150 Massachusetts Avenue and the creation of new classroooms and practice rooms campuswide. It is hoped the expansion and renovations will meet Berklee's needs well into the next century.

Amar Bose, President Berk, and Oleta Adams.

The 1994-95 academic year started with singer/songwriter Oleta Adams, a two-time Grammy nominee for her hit singles "Get Here" and "Don't Let the Sun Go Down on Me," and Amar G. Bose, Chair of the Board and Technical Director of the BOSE Corporation, receiving honorary degrees at the 1994 Entering Student Convocation.

1995 John Zorn's Masada releases four CDs.   James Carter releases *The Real Quiet Storm*.   Jacky Terresson releases *Jacky Terresson*.   Joe Henderson releases *Double Rainbow*.

1995 Hootie and the Blowfish release *Cracked Rear View*.   Neil Young and Pearl Jam release *Mirror Ball*.   TLC goes platinum with *CrazySexyCool*.   Jerry Garcia dies.

Natalie Cole joins Stefanie Kelly '95 on stage during the 1995 Commencement concert.

Mrs. Susan G. Berk, President Berk, and James Taylor.

At its 50th anniversary year Commencement in May 1995, Berklee bestowed honorary degrees on singer/songwriter James Taylor, singer Natalie Cole, and retiring Berklee professor Herb Pomeroy. The daughter of singer and pianist Nat King Cole, Cole has won 11 Grammy Awards, including seven for her 1991 tribute to her late father, *Unforgettable with Love*. James Taylor, also a multiple Grammy winner, has topped the charts for over 30 years with gold- and platinum-selling singles such as "Fire and Rain," "You've Got a Friend," and a remake of the Motown classic "How Sweet It Is."

In his Commencement address, Taylor said that music "reminds us of the truth that lies beneath and beyond the illusion that we live in. It gives us relief from the insanity of constantly trying to invent ourselves. And in this way, music is pure spiritual practice. I thank God for music, and I thank music for God."

Mrs. Susan G. Berk (second from left) with her daughters Nancy (left) and Lucy, and B.J. Ramone (right), son of producer Phil Ramone, at the 1995 Commencement reception.

Herb Pomeroy leads the Concert Jazz Orchestra at the
1995 Commencement concert.

Herb Pomeroy performs with Joe Hunt on drums and John Repucci on bass at the Herb Pomeroy Tribute Concert.

At the Herb Pomeroy Tribute, Chancellor Lawrence Berk is joined by Joe Viola, Alice Viola, and Herb Pomeroy.

After 40 years at Berklee, Herb Pomeroy retired from teaching in 1995. The college marked the departure of one of its most revered teachers with a tribute concert in April 1995. An all-star line-up of former students joined Pomeroy and his 1994-95 Concert Jazz Orchestra for an evening of music and reminiscences. Guest soloists and composers, including John Abercrombie, Toshiko Akiyoshi, Michael Gibbs, Abraham Laboriel, Sr., Rob Mounsey '75, Tiger Okoshi, Tommy Smith '86, Sadao Watanabe, and Joe Zawinul, flew in from around the world. From the Berklee community, concert producer Gary Burton was a featured soloist, and Greg Hopkins shared conducting duties on his piece "Inner Voyage." Arif Mardin contributed "Tone Poem for Herbie," a composition written especially for the occassion. To round out the special evening, Pomeroy and a faculty trio of Ray Santisi, John Repucci, and Joe Hunt performed two numbers from the Ellington/Strayhorn repertoire.

Praise for Pomeroy's unique gifts as a teacher and anecdotes from the classroom and the bandstand punctuated the music. "Herb can play what he teaches, and teach what he plays," said Gary Burton, one of the evening's several speakers, which included Arif Mardin, emcee Larry Monroe, and President Lee Eliot Berk.

In the decades during which Pomeroy was a member of the Berklee community, much had changed at the college and in music and music education. But some things had also endured. The creativity of Berklee students and faculty, their willingness to innovate, and their love for music have remained a constant for half a century. It is a spirit perhaps best summarized in remarks founder and Chanceller Lawrence Berk made in 1966, when as president he dedicated the college's new building at 1140 Boylston Street: "Our aim is to build a school that will never know completion," he said, "but will continually advance to meet the growing needs of the world of music."

Special guests at the Herb Pomeroy Tribute Concert (left to right) Arif Mardin, Sadao Watanabe, Rob Mounsey, Toshiko Akiyoshi, Greg Hopkins, John Abercrombie, Gary Burton, Ray Santisi, Tommy Smith, Abraham Laboriel, Sr., Magali Souriau, Michael Gibbs, Tiger Okoshi, Joe Zawinul, Herb Pomeroy, Tommy Kamp, Joe Hunt, and John Repucci.

They performed along with the Concert Jazz Orchestra: Pete Rende '95, piano; Christian Fast '95, guitar; David Wiesner '94, bass; Sebastiaan De Krom, drums; Taku Hirano '95 and Bertram Lehmann '94, percussion; Bill Vint, Ignaz Dinné, Christopher Hollyday, Jeff Ellwood, and Ryan Shore, saxophones; Richard Nant '95, Brad Mason '95, Staffan Jonsson '95, Justin Mullens, trumpets; Elliot Mason,

Recording Credits

Berklee began releasing recordings of our outstanding student performers and writers starting in the mid-1950s with the 15-volume series of *Jazz in the Classroom* LP/score sets. Then, as now, the mission of the college was to share information about jazz, and the LP/score publications were seen as important new means of doing so. Musicians and educators from all over the world were given the then unusual opportunity of studying compositional, arranging, and performance techniques from the scores provided with the recorded music, and many were the future renowned professionals who were given their first visibility as students in this series—figures like Toshiko Akiyoshi, Arif Mardin, Sadao Watanabe, and Joe Zawinul.

As the college's technical facilities evolved, the college continued the tradition with a radio series distributed around the United States called "Jazzbeat from Berklee." Since the late 1980s, the college has produced one or more compact discs each year featuring a variety of student groups and music ranging in style from jazz to pop.

Today, our ensemble program offerings cover extensive territory including small and large groups, instrumental and vocal, and representing many styles from funk to gospel to big band. Berklee arrangers and composers contribute most of the material, and CDs produced by the college for release each year are recorded in the college's Music Production and Engineering Department studios.

The most enduring impression I have after more than 30 years of being part of Berklee is the continuing cast of talented musicians that comes through the institution. Listening to the highlights of these Berklee studio sessions recorded over the years makes me very proud of our many graduates. Our student population is now about 40 percent international, and even on the earliest recordings from Berklee, you will notice names of students from many different countries around the world. Our young musicians' skill and creativity are a constant reminder that the future of music is in good hands.

Gary Burton
Dean of Curriculum '62

Jazz in the Classroom Volume I

Amber's Folly 4:56

composer	**Kenton Morrow**
arranger	**Kenton Morrow**
soloist	**Paul Fontaine**

Silhouette 2:53

composer	**Toshiko Akiyoshi**
arranger	**Toshiko Akiyoshi**

collective student personnel

composer/arranger	**Toshiko Akiyoshi**
composer/arranger/ piano	**Charles Bechler, Jr.**
alto saxophone	**Anthony Bisazza**
drums	**William Briggs**
tenor saxophone	**Gordon Brisker**
bass	**Joseph Cardinale**
trumpet	**William Chase**
trombone	**Joseph Ciavardone**
trombone/bass trumpet	**Roger Delillo**
guitar	**Joseph Egidio**
trumpet	**Paul Fontaine**
piano	**Harold Galper**
drums	**Les Harris**
trumpet	**John Hening**
composer/arranger	**Gene Langdoc**
trombone	**William Legan**
composer/arranger/ alto saxophone	**Kenton Morrow**
composer/arranger/alto, baritone saxophone	**James Mosher**
trumpet	**Daniel Nolan, Jr.**
trumpet	**Lester Powell**
composer/arranger	**William St. Laurent**
tenor saxophone	**Dodge Terlemezian**
conductor	**Herb Pomeroy**

Jazz in the Classroom Volume II

Yesteryears 3:20

composer	**Arif Mardin**
arranger	**Arif Mardin**
soloist	**Charlie Mariano**

The Long Wait 4:59

composer	**Arif Mardin**
arranger	**Arif Mardin**
soloists	**Nicholas Brignola**
	Edwin Morgan
	Robert James
	Gabor Szabo
	Gene Cherico

collective student personnel

composer/arranger	**Toshiko Akiyoshi**
trumpet	**Edward Armour**
composer/arranger/ piano	**Charles Bechler**
alto saxophone	**Anthony Bisazza**
baritone saxophone	**Nicholas Brignola**
drums	**Harry Brown**
bass	**Gene Cherico**
trumpet	**John Hening**
composer/arranger/ piano	**Robert James**
trombone	**Paul McLeod**
composer/arranger	**Arif Mardin**
trombone	**Edwin Morgan**
trumpet	**Daniel Nolan, Jr.**
tenor saxophone	**Anthony Osiecki**
composer/arranger	**James Progris**
vibraphone	**Monty Stark**
guitar	**Gabor Szabo**
tenor saxophone	**Dodge Terlemezian**
trumpet	**John Weaver**
trombone	**Jack Wertheimer**
composer/arranger/ bass trumpet	**Richard Wright**
piano	**Joe Zawinul**

faculty personnel

conductor	**Herb Pomeroy**
lead alto	**Charlie Mariano**
lead trumpet	**Everett Longstreth**

Jazz in the Classroom Volume V: A Tribute to Benny Golson

I Remember Clifford 4:19

composer	Benny Golson
arranger	Don French
soloist	Gary Burton

collective student personnel

drums	Francis "Butch" Axsmith
bass	Pearson Beckwith
trumpet	Robert Bockholt
vibraphone/piano/ arranger	Gary Burton
tenor saxophone/flute	Ted Casher
drums	Tom Check
trombone	Keith Davy
arranger	Don French
conga drum	William Fitch
trombone/arranger	Michael Gibbs
trumpet/arranger	Paul Kelly
trumpet	Fred Lesher
tenor saxophone	Steve Marcus
trumpet	Dan Nolan
piano	Edward Saldanha
baritone saxophone/ arranger	Robert Seastrom
drums	Petar Spassov
alto saxophone	Jack Stevens
bass/arranger	Tony Teixeira
tenor saxophone	Barry Ulman
trumpet	Alan Ware
arranger	Clifford Weeks
trombone	Kenneth Wenzel

faculty personnel

conductor	Herb Pomeroy
lead trumpet	Everett Longstreth
lead alto	Dick Johnson

Jazz in the Classroom Volume VI: A Tribute to Quincy Jones

Stockholm Sweetnin' 3:43

composer	Quincy Jones
arranger	MIchael Gibbs
soloists	Dusan Gojkovic
	John Scott

Meet Benny Baily 3:48

composer	Quincy Jones
arranger	Chris Swanson
soloists	Steve Marcus
	Chris Swanson

Change of Pace 3:50

composer	Quincy Jones
arranger	Michael Gibbs
soloists	Gary Burton
	Dusan Gojkovic

collective student personnel

alto saxophone/clarinet	Heinz Bigler
trumpet/French horn	Robert Bockholt
vibraphone/piano	Gary Burton
trumpet	Dave Ferguson
trombone/arranger	Michael Gibbs
trumpet/flugelhorn	Dusan Gojkovic
bass	Don Jones
soprano, tenor saxophone	Steve Marcus
baritone saxophone/ bass clarinet	Ken Mamayek
drums	Dan Martin
piano	Mike Nock
piano	Pat Pratta
tenor saxophone/ clarinet	Ralph Rayner
bass trombone	Tony Salvatori
trumpet	Tony Scodwell
trumpet	John Scott
alto saxophone/clarinet	Jack Stevens
valve trombone/ trombonium/piano	Chris Swansen
trombone	Ken Wenzel
bass	Dave Young

faculty personnel

conductor	Herb Pomeroy
lead trumpet	Everett Longstreth

Jazz in the Classroom Volume VIII

Upper Manhattan Medical Group 4:25

composer	Billy Strayhorn
arranger	Al Feeny
soloist	Sadao Watanabe

Falling Like a Raindrop 4:21

composer	Duke Ellington
arranger	Gene Perla
soloist	Sadao Watanabe

collective student personnel

alto saxophone/flute	Anthony Baker
baritone saxophone/ clarinet/bass clarinet	Errol Burke
trumpet	Jim Castaldi
arranger	Graham Collier
trombone	Steve Cox
piano	Bob Deagan
bass trombone	Steve Devich
tenor saxophone	Alex Elin
piano/arranger	Al Feeny
arranger	Emin Findikoglu
trumpet	Dale Frank
trumpet/arranger	Milt Freiberg
tenor saxophone/ clarinet/arranger	Bennett Friedman
trombone	Mike Gibbs
trumpet	Larry Gilbo
bass	Lenny Harlos
trumpet	Roland Ligart
bass	Bud Mardin
trombone	Karl McDannell
tenor saxophone/ clarinet	Hal McIntyre
trumpet	Wes Nicholas
alto saxophone/clarinet	Charles Owens
drums/arranger	Ted Pease
piano/arranger	Gene Perla
trumpet/flugelhorn	Skip Potter
piano/arranger	Mike Rendish
piano	Mike Renzi
trombone	Barry Ross
drums	Ted Sajdyk
drums	Bill Theile
alto saxophone/flute	Sadao Watanabe
tenor saxophone/ clarinet	Ford Winner
conductor	Herb Pomeroy

Jazz in the Classroom Volume IX: A Tribute to Oliver Nelson

Anacrusis 3:20

composer	Oliver Nelson
arranger	Joze Privsek
soloists	Sadao Watanabe,
	Erroll Burke

collective student personnel

tenor saxophone/ clarinet/bass clarinet	Erroll Burke
bass	Kent Carter
trumpet	Jim Castaldi
French horn	Alf Clausen
trombone	Jerry Collins
bass trombone	Steve Devich
trombone	Tony DiMaggio
tenor saxophone	Alex Elin
trumpet	Dale Frank
baritone, tenor saxophone/flute	Gerry Geiger
arranger	John Julian
trumpet	Roland Ligart
arranger	John McGill
tenor saxophone/ clarinet	Hal McIntyre
trumpet	Mike Mantler
alto saxophone/ flute/alto flute	Jimmy Mosher
trumpet	Wes Nicholas
alto saxophone/flute	Charles Owens
piano/bass/arranger	Gene Perla
trumpet	Michael Price
arranger	Joze Privesk
piano/arranger	Mike Rendish
trumpet	Dick Robilotto
drums	Ted Sajdyk
drums	Bill Thiele
alto saxophone/ flute/arranger	Sadao Watanabe
trumpet	George Zonce
conductor	Herb Pomeroy

Jazz in the Classroom
Volume X:
A Tribute to Charlie Mariano

Iberian Waltz   4:26

composer	Charlie Mariano
arranger	John McGill
soloists	Ernie Watts
	George Zonce

collective student personnel

guitar	John Abercrombie
trombone/arranger	Nicholas Aksionczyk
bass	Yasuo Arakawa
drums	John Betsch
trumpet	Lin Biviano
drums	George Bookataub
trombone	Sam Burtis
piano	Charles Cassara
trumpet	James Castaldi
French horn/arranger	Alf Clausen
trombone	Jerry Collins
bass	John Curzio
alto saxophone/flute	Thomas Delaney
trombone	Tony DiMaggio
trumpet	Darryl Eaton
tenor saxophone	Ed Fiorenza
vibraphone	Brian Cascoigne
tenor saxophone/flute	Gerald Geiger
bass	Nate Hygelund
piano	John Julian
bass	Marshall Mardin
tenor saxophone/ arranger	John McGill
piano/arranger	Michel Mention
baritone saxophone/ flute/clarinet/ bass clarinet	Allen Michalek
guitar	Joe Miller
bass	William Moulton
tenor saxophone/ clarinet	Roger Neumann
trumpet	Wesley Nicholas
trumpet	Michael Price
piano/arranger	Michael Rendish
trumpet	Dick Robilotto
tenor saxophone/ clarinet	Alan Rowe
trombone	Jules Rowell
drums	Ted Sajdyk
piano/arranger	Carlton Schroeder
alto saxophone/clarinet	Joseph Seidman
alto saxophone/ flute/arranger	Sadao Watanabe
alto saxophone/flute	Ernie Watts
trumpet	George Zonce
conductor	Herb Pomeroy

Jazz in the Classroom
Volume XI:
Jazz Internationale

Hatho Thingald   4:32

composer	Traditional
arranger	Dave Mott
soloist	Charlie Mariano

collective student personnel

trombone	Nick Aksionczyk
bass	Yasuo Arakawa
trumpet	Lin Biviano
piano	Alan Broadbent
trombone/tuba	Sam Burtis
drums	Artie Cabral
arranger	Charlie Cassara
trumpet	Jim Castaldi
arranger/French horn flugelhorn/trumpet/ arranger	Alf Clausen
trombone	Dave Danenberg
trumpet	Tony DiMaggio
tenor saxophone/ arranger	Darryl Eaton
bass	Gerry Geiger
arranger/piano	Calvin Hill
drums	Mike Hughes
flute/clarinet/ tenor saxophone	Joe LaBarbera
bass	Pat LaBarbera
drums	Daniel Lessard
trombone	Harvey Mason
baritone saxophone	Dave Matlock
trombone arranger/baritone saxophone/bass clarinet arranger/tenor saxophone/clarinet	Al Michalek
baritone saxophone	Wayne Mogul
trumpet	Dave Mott
trumpet	Roger Neumann
trombone	John Oslawski
drums	Pete Pantaluk
alto saxophone/ flute/arranger arranger/ tenor saxophone	Mike Price
bass	Jules Rowell
alto saxophone/flute	Ted Sajdyk
drums	Joe Seidman
trumpet	John Shaw
	Miroslav Vitous
	Ernie Watts
	Chip White
	George Zonce
conductor	Herb Pomeroy

Jazz in the Classroom
Volume XII

Ages Ago   5:34

composer	Alan Broadbent
arranger	Alan Broadbent
soloist	Alex Elin

collective student personnel

trumpet/flugelhorn	Robert Agnew
bass	Yasuo Arakawa
tenor saxophone/ clarinet/arranger	Gary Anderson
trumpet	James Bossert
drums	Jeffrey Brillinger
piano/arranger	Alan Broadbent
trombone	Samuel Burtis
drums	Artie Cabral
alto saxophone/ oboe/flute	Richard Centalonza
trombone	Andrew Cohen
alto saxophone/ clarinet/flute	Richard Cole
trumpet/flugelhorn/ arranger	David Danenberg
trumpet	Stanton Davis, Jr.
trumpet	Jay DeWald
piano	Harvey Diamond
bass clarinet	Harry Drabkin
trumpet	Darryl K. Eaton

tenor saxophone	Alex Elin
tenor saxophone/ clarinet/flute/arranger	Edward Fiorenza
trombone	Larry Fisher
trombone	Mike Gibson
drums	Arthur Gore
bass	Calvin Hill
arranger	Michael Hughes
trumpet/flugelhorn/ arranger	Rolf Johnson
tenor saxophone/flute	Pat LaBarbera
trombone	Anthony Lada
bass	Rick Laird
piano	Cedric Lawson
trombone	David Matlock
trombone	Wayne Mogel
alto saxophone/clarinet baritone saxophone/ bass clarinet	Larry Monroe
bass	Dave Mott
baritone saxophone/ bass clarinet	Jiri Mraz
tenor saxophone/ clarinet/arranger	Barrie Nettles
French horn	Roger Neumann
trumpet	Stanley Opatka
trumpet	Peter Pantaluk
trumpet	Mike Price
drums	Larry Pyatt
arranger	Eugene Roma
trombone	Masaniko Satoa
alto saxophone/clarinet	James Seaman
trombone	Joe Seldman
trombone	Rick Stepton
bass	Jason Stock
trumpet/arranger	Miroslav Vitous
trumpet	Jack Walrath
	George Zonce
ensemble coach	Herb Pomeroy

Jazz in the Classroom
Volume XIII

Jacob's Tailor	5:58

composer	Jaxon Stock
arranger	Jaxon Stock
soloist	Robert Sommers

Snaggin' Song	4:19

composer	Jaxon Stock
arranger	Jaxon Stock
soloist	Hal Crook

collective student personnel

alto saxophone/flute	Gary Anderson
bass	Richard Appleman
trumpet	Franklin Biviano
trumpet	Sauber Cantees
alto saxophone/oboe	Richard Caruso
trumpet	Dennis Collier
trombone	Hal Crook
trumpet	Jay Dewald
baritone saxophone/ bass clarinet	Howard Drye
piano	John Ferrara
tenor saxophone/flute	Ed Fiorenza
trombone	William Gemmer
trombone	Rod Hansen
trumpet/flugelhorn	Daniel Hayes
trombone	Ludvig Hinrichs
French horn	Jonathan Klein
piano	George McFettridge
trombone	Barry Mertz
alto saxophone/clarinet	Larry Monroe
tenor saxophone/flute	Eric Naismith
bass	John Neves
trombone	Steve Nilson
trumpet	Peter Pantaluk
alto saxophone/ clarinet/flute	Jim Perry
trumpet	Ralph Rickert
trumpet	Claudio Roditi
bass	Harvie Swartz
tenor saxophone/ clarinet	Michael Scorah
drums	Ted Seibs
drums	Greg Soininen
trumpet/flugelhorn	Robert Sommers
tenor saxophone/flute	Salvatore Spicola
trombone	Jaxon Stock
piano	Al Ulanowsky
piano	Vicki Von Eps
baritone saxophone/ bass clarinet	Richard Wald
drums	Grayling Wallace
trombone	Ron Wetzel

ensemble coach	Herb Pomeroy

Jazz in the Classroom
Volume XIV

Paper Dragon	3:38

composer	Rob Mounsey
arranger	Rob Mounsey
soloist	Alan Zavod

collective student personnel

reeds	Justo Almario
bass	Chris Amberger
bass	Rich Appleman
drums	Harry Blazer
French horn	John Clark
trumpet	Dennis Collier
arranger/composer	John Damian
trumpet	Dave Danenberg
reeds	Bill Drewes
trumpet	Dave Dubinsky
reeds	Rob Eldridge
trombone	Paul Frederick
trumpet	Frank Grasso
trombone	Rod Hansen
arranger/composer	Axel Jungbluth
trumpet/arranger/ composer	George McFetridge
arranger/composer	Rob Mounsey
reeds	Dennis Muffley
French horn	Stanley Opatka
trombone	Keith O'Quinn
reeds	Jim Perry
reeds	Bill Pierce
horn	Rob Probst French
trumpet	Larry Pyatt
trumpet	Herb Roberston
guitar	John Scofield
drums	Ted Seibs
trombone	Larry Shunk
trumpet	Steve Veikley
reeds	Harvey Wainapel
piano	Ken Werner
trombone	Dennis Wilson
piano	Alan Zavod

ensemble coach	Herb Pomeroy

Jazz in the Classroom
Volume XV

By Gone	5:04

composer	Tiger Okoshi
arranger	Tiger Okoshi

collective student personnel

reeds	Les Arbuckle
trombone	Steve Bulla
trumpet	Tim Burke
trumpet	Ken Cervenka
trombone	Kim Cissel
trombone	Harold Clark
guitar	Joe Cohn
trumpet	Jeff Conrad
trumpet	Jeff Davis
reeds	Nelson Dellamaggiore
drums	Kenwood Dennard
trombone	Glenn Franke
reeds	Orpheus Gaitanopoulos
reeds	Jim Germann
piano	Yaron Gershovski
guitar	Jamie Glaser
trumpet	William Glenister
trumpet	Mac Gollehon
reeds	Jim Grantham
piano	Eric Gunnison
trombone	Kevin Haines
drums	Guy Hayat
guitar	Richard Hohenberger
trombone	Roger Homefield
trombone	Jeff Huffnagle
reeds	Dan Klimoski
trumpet	Marc Kupferberg
trombone	Nick Lane
reeds	Michael Lawrence
bass	John Lockwood
reeds	Eric Marienthal
reeds	Yoshi Maruta
reeds	Berke McKelvey
trumpet	Rick Miller
trombone	David Mills
reeds	Paul Moen
trumpet	Larry Moses
trumpet	Wayne Naus
reeds	Doug Norwine
piano	Richard Odgren
reeds	Akira Ohmori
trumpet	Tiger Okoshi
piano	Mike Pellera
reeds	James Perry
drums	Roberto Petaccia
reeds	Olivier Peters
trombone	Lenny Peterson
trombone	Robert Pilkington
trombone	Kai Poscente
trumpet	Ken Pullig
trombone	Sal Randazzo
bass	Rodrigo Saenz
drums	Jun Saito
trumpet	Haruyuki Sawada
reeds	Guri Teuschler
trumpet	Chaya Tinterow
reeds	Akio Ueda

ensemble coach	Herb Pomeroy

Remastered from the original master tapes by Joe Hostetter, January 1995.

Vocal Jazz Ensemble

Night and Day 4:28
Cole Porter -
Horns, Inc., ASCAP

Summertime 5:23
George Gershwin -
Chappel & Co., Inc. &
Gershwin Publishing Corp., ASCAP

Rain Waltz 4:47
Fred Hersch -
Fred Hersch Music, BMI

If I Fell 3:40
Paul McCartney,
John Lennon -
Maclen Music, EMI Unart, BMI

directed by | April Arabian
sopranos | Yuka Hata
| Holly Palmer
altos | Kira McConaghy
| Kemba Francis
tenors | Leland Simmons
| Tommy Kamp
basses | Gray Gillian
| Dennis Williams, Jr.
alto saxophone | Joe Cunningham
piano | Mercedes Rossy
keyboards | Barry D.
guitar | Mark Cox
bass | Hans Glawischnig
drums | Marc Miralta
produced by | April Arabian
engineer | Robin Coxe-Yeldman
assistant engineers | Jay Jennings
| Alvaro De Alencar
| Scott Cannizzaro
| Andrew Schulz

Recorded in Studio A, Berklee College of Music

Thelonious Monk Ensemble

Evidence 6:00
Thelonious Monk -
Thelonious Music, BMI

Trinkle Tinkle 4:00
Thelonious Monk -
Thelonious Music, BMI

Humph/Epistrophy 6:00
Thelonious Monk -
Thelonious Music, BMI

directed by | Rick Peckham
trumpet | David Boato
tenor saxophone | Dave Barraza
| Teodross Avery
piano | Pamela Butchart
guitar | Niclas Knudson
bass | Jeff Hill
drums | Blake Lindberg
produced by | Rick Peckham
engineer | John Servies
assistant engineer | Alvaro De Alencar

Recorded in Studio B, Berklee College of Music

Concert Jazz Orchestra

Little African Flower 8:19
Duke Ellington -
Tempo Music, Inc., ASCAP

Mineur 5:13
Michel Barbaud -
Marseilles, France

Own Legs 4:40
Lars Lindvall - Kisa, Sweden

directed by | Herb Pomeroy
trumpets | Keiichi Hashimoto
| Tom Hovey
| Gary Loruuso
| Lars Lindvall
trombones | Andreas Mittermayer
| Dan Fox
| Hikaru Tsukamoto
alto saxophones | Joe Cunningham
| Pat Loomis
baritone saxophone | Erik Gibb
tenor saxophones | Dave Barraza
| Seamus Blake
piano | Mercedes Rossy
guitar | Sten Hostfalt
electric bass | Yorai Oron
drums | Marc Miralta
produced by | Herb Pomeroy
engineer | Joe Hostetter
assistant engineers | Robert Toledo
| Griff Peters

Recorded in Studio A, Berklee College of Music

Reverence Gospel Ensemble

He's Been Faithful 4:10
Carol Cymbala -
Word Music, Inc., ASCAP

He Has It In Control 5:45
Dennis Montgomery III - BMI

**Jesus Will See
You Through** 4:19
Dennis Montgomery III - BMI

**Over and Over He
Keeps On Blessing Me** 5:43
Darius Brooks -
Word Music, Inc., ASCAP

directed by | Orville Wright
altos | La Quinta J. Brown
| Deleska Crockett
| Donica D. Holmes
| Sharine Janse
| Kerri Little
| Rotonja Rogers
| Yoshiko Saita
| Denise Stephens
| Nicole Anne Williams
baritones | Richard L. D'Abreau Jr.
| Andrew J. Dorsett
| John Ed McGurk
| Derrick Young
basses | Kevin Marren
| Dan Williams
sopranos | Chelsea Bailey
| Kimberly C. Banks
| Eve Buigues
| Stacey Huggins
| Jodi Jenkins
| Gwendolyn Leathers
| Angelena Payne
| Robin K. Spears
| Lesley White
| Tamika Young
tenors | Daniel L. Curry
| DeMann
| Michael Hamilton
| Chris Lambert
| Richard K. Meffley
| Veit Renn
| Jonathan Royal
| Leland J. Simmons
| Michael Torino
| Trammel
produced by | Orville Wright
engineer | Carl Beatty
assistant engineers | James Saez
| Greg Kalember

Recorded in Studio A, Berklee College of Music

About the Author

Ed Hazell is coauthor with Lewis Porter and Michael Ullman of *Jazz: From Its Origins to the Present* and is a contributing editor to the *New Grove Dictionary of Jazz*. His articles about jazz have appeared in the *Boston Phoenix*, the *Boston Globe*, *Cadence*, *Coda*, *Modern Drummer*, and other publications.

Acknowledgements

Funding for *Berklee: The First Fifty Years* was provided by the Lawrence and Alma Berk Fund and the Lee and Susan Berk Fund at Berklee, with additional support from EMCO Printers and KAO Infosystems.

Berklee gratefully acknowledges the work of the following photographers:
Parker Bartlett, Allen Bush, Kimberly Grant, Rob Hayes, Rob Hochschild, Bob Kramer, Joji Sawa, Keith Sipes, Bill Wasserman, and all of the photographers who have worked for Berklee over the years who could not be identified. Special thanks to the Boston Public Library Print Department.

Disc One

1. **Amber's Folly**   4:56
   Kenton Morrow

2. **Silhouette**   2:53
   Toshiko Akiyoshi

3. **Yesteryears**   3:20
   Arif Mardin

4. **The Long Wait**   4:59
   Arif Mardin

5. **I Remember Clifford**   4:19
   Benny Golson

6. **Stockholm Sweetnin'**   3:43
   Quincy Jones

7. **Meet Benny Baily**   3:48
   Quincy Jones

8. **Change of Pace**   3:50
   Quincy Jones

9. **Upper Manhattan
   Medical Group**   4:25
   Billy Strayhorn

10. **Falling Like a Raindrop**   4:21
    Duke Ellington

11. **Anacrusis**   3:20
    Oliver Nelson

12. **Iberian Waltz**   4:26
    Charlie Mariano

13. **Hatho Thingald**   4:29
    Traditional

14. **Ages Ago**   5:30
    Alan Broadbent

15. **Jacob's Tailor**   5:59
    Jaxon Stock

16. **Snaggin' Song**   4:19
    Jaxon Stock

17. **Paper Dragon**   3:38
    Rob Mounsey

18. **By Gone**   5:04
    Tiger Okoshi

Disc Two

1. **Night and Day**   4:28
   Cole Porter

2. **Summertime**   5:23
   George Gershwin

3. **Rain Waltz**   4:47
   Fred Hersch

4. **If I Fell**   3:40
   Paul McCartney
   John Lennon

5. **Evidence**   6:00
   Thelonious Monk

6. **Trinkle Tinkle**   4:00
   Thelonious Monk

7. **Humph/Epistrophy**   6:00
   Thelonious Monk

8. **Little African Flower**   8:19
   Duke Ellington

9. **Mineur**   5:13
   Michel Barbaud

10. **Own Legs**   4:40
    Lars Lindvall

11. **He's Been Faithful**   4:10
    Carol Cymbala

12. **He Has It In Control**   5:45
    Dennis Montgomery III

13. **Jesus Will See
    You Through**   4:19
    Dennis Montgomery III

14. **Over and Over He
    Keeps On Blessing Me**   5:43
    Darius Brooks